Faculty
MENTORING

Booklets for Mentors and Mentees

Available Exclusively From www.Styluspub.com

While we afford quantity discounts for bulk purchases of *Faculty Mentoring* (see copyright page for details), we also offer the option of buying Chapters 1 and 3 as individual e-booklets. Each respectively provides a succinct summary of the roles and expectations of Mentor and Mentee.

Faculty Mentoring / Mentor Guide

Comprises the following materials from *Faculty Mentoring*:

- Chapter 1, "Tips for Mentors Inside or Outside the Department"

And from the appendices:
- New Faculty Mentoring Program Statement of Commitment and Confidentiality
- Needs Assessment for New Faculty
- Five-Year Tenure Preparation Plan

Faculty Mentoring / Mentee Guide

Comprises the following materials from *Faculty Mentoring*:

- Chapter 3, "New Faculty Tips on Having a Successful Mentoring Experience"

And from the appendices:
- New Faculty Mentoring Program Statement of Commitment and Confidentiality
- Needs Assessment for New Faculty
- Five-Year Tenure Preparation Plan

These affordably priced booklets are intended for individual purchase by mentors and mentees. They are available exclusively through the Stylus Publishing website, www.Styluspub.com, and are supplied in two digital formats: EPUB and PDF (compatible with any PC or Mac with Adobe Digital Editions installed, and any Android or iOS device with an Adobe DRM–compliant reading app installed). Each booklet may be downloaded on up to six devices.

Faculty
MENTORING

A Practical Manual for Mentors, Mentees, Administrators, and Faculty Developers

Susan L. Phillips

and

Susan T. Dennison

Foreword by Milton D. Cox

Stylus

STERLING, VIRGINIA

COPYRIGHT © 2015 BY
STYLUS PUBLISHING, LLC

Published by Stylus Publishing, LLC
22883 Quicksilver Drive
Sterling, Virginia 20166-2102

Library of Congress Cataloging-in-Publication Data
Phillips, Susan L.
  Faculty mentoring : a practical manual for mentors, mentees,
administrators, and faculty developers / Susan L. Phillips and Susan
T. Dennison ; foreword by Milton D. Cox.
    pages cm
Includes bibliographical references and index.
ISBN 978-1-62036-171-9 (cloth : alk. paper)
ISBN 978-1-62036-172-6 (pbk. : alk. paper)
ISBN 978-1-62036-173-3 (library networkable e-edition)
ISBN 978-1-62036-174-0 (consumer e-edition) 1. Mentoring in
education. 2. College teachers–In-service training. I. Title.
  LB1731.4.P54 2014
  371.102--dc23
                                                                  2014016896

13-digit ISBN: 978-1-62036-171-9 (cloth)
13-digit ISBN: 978-1-62036-172-6 (paperback)
13-digit ISBN: 978-1-62036-173-3 (library networkable e-edition)
13-digit ISBN: 978-1-62036-174-0 (consumer e-edition)

Printed in the United States of America

All first editions printed on acid-free paper
that meets the American National Standards Institute
Z39-48 Standard.

Bulk Purchases

Quantity discounts are available for use in
workshops and for staff development.
Call 1-800-232-0223

First Edition, 2015

10 9 8 7 6 5 4 3 2 1

To all the faculty, staff, and administrators whose commitment made the UNCG New Faculty Mentoring Program a successful reality, and from whom we have learned so much.

Contents

Foreword   ix
Milton D. Cox

Acknowledgments   xv

Introduction: Overview and Purpose of the Manual   1

1 **Tips for Mentors Inside or Outside the Department**   5

2 **Guidelines for Setting Up, Planning, and Facilitating a Mentoring Group**   11

3 **New Faculty Tips on Having a Successful Mentoring Experience**   21

4 **Tips for Guidance of Departmental Mentoring**   27

5 **Guidelines for Administrators**   35

6 **Advice for the Director of a Faculty Mentoring Program**   41

7 **Review of Mentoring in the Higher Education Literature**   47

Appendices
APPENDIX A *Books and Web Resources*   59
APPENDIX B *Relationship-Building Exercises*   65
APPENDIX C *Active Mentoring Worksheets*   71
APPENDIX D *Closure Activities*   77
APPENDIX E *Group Mentoring Materials*   81
APPENDIX F *Program Implementation Materials*   87
APPENDIX G *Program Assessment Materials*   99
APPENDIX H *Department-Level Materials*   107
APPENDIX I *Sample Program Documents*   117

About the Authors   125

Index   127

Foreword

For 50 years, as both an instructor and educational developer in higher education, it has been my pleasure to observe, engage, and guide faculty mentoring of students and colleagues. My choice for mentoring approaches has been group mentoring, a topic covered excellently in chapter 2 of this book. Mentoring in and by groups has worked effectively in my years of experience in higher education, and what was surprising at first but clear in the following years was the similarity of successful group mentoring strategies and outcomes for both students and faculty (Cox, 2009). Effective mentoring occurs by building community and nurturing learning and scholarship within both groups. I share now my stories of development in hopes that you will recognize and seize similar opportunities.

In 1970, as director of undergraduate studies and chief departmental advisor in mathematics at Miami University, I was invited to be the advisor of the Miami chapter of Pi Mu Epsilon, the national mathematics honor society. Although I was not aware of the term at the time, I found that fostering a *student learning community* was the first step in mentoring within a student group. What worked well included providing a combination of pizza and productive seminars. The next step was to provide an opportunity for students to present their investigations, and in 1974 we developed a regional student conference (still in place) to enable this to happen (Cox, 1977). After this initial success, we received support to fund our student presenters at the national summer mathematics meetings, and this led to traveling in the summers by van or train to the likes of Portland, Toronto, and San Francisco, thus building even stronger student community. The final step in this developmental process toward scholarship

was mentoring students who had made presentations to publish them in the *Pi Mu Epsilon Journal.*

This story was about a special group of students. However, in my classes for all students I have used cooperative learning groups to provide group mentoring in order to enable learning. Developing each small classroom group into a mini student learning community has enhanced the learning of students and built community in my classes. I always keep in mind the findings of the study by Johnson, Johnson, and Smith (1998):

> Since 1898 there have been over 600 experimental and over 100 correlational studies of cooperative, competitive, and individualistic efforts. These studies show that cooperation, compared with competitive and individualistic efforts, typically results in greater efforts to achieve, more positive relationships among students, and greater psychological health. (pp. 1.15–1.16)

In my case, reducing math anxiety by engaging group work was a big step toward enhancing learning.

As a faculty member deeply involved in the silo of my discipline, how did I discover and learn about student learning communities, cooperative learning, and mentoring?

At this point my curiosity led me to refocus my academic career. In 1980 I was invited to direct Miami's Lilly Endowment–funded Post-Doctoral Teaching Awards Program that provided a venue for learning about teaching for early-career faculty (Cox, 1995). My new-faculty colleagues and I became students, and I engaged this opportunity to find perspectives and evidence about what worked with respect to group mentoring. The way we developed this program was to build community each year in the group of 8 to 10 new colleagues by eating well; traveling by train to conferences; and incubating a scholarship in which these junior faculty members designed, implemented, and assessed teaching and learning projects (Cox, 2003). That led to their engagement in what Boyer (1990) called the scholarship of teaching and learning. To provide a forum to present their work, in 1981 we developed the Lilly Conference on College Teaching, now in its 34th year; and in 1990 founded a refereed journal in which to publish this scholarship, the *Journal on Excellence in College Teaching*. These efforts were made not just for Miami's faculty, but for all colleagues in higher education. My mentoring role was extended to aspiring faculty presenters and authors. It was at this point that the authors of this book contacted me to present some sessions about mentoring on their campus as they were designing their program. I am pleased to see this book as a productive outcome of their efforts.

The same strategies that worked for group mentoring of students have worked for group mentoring of early-career faculty. This has taken place in the faculty learning communities that I have facilitated for 35 years (Cox, 1995, 1997).

Group mentoring also works well in faculty learning communities with membership populated by faculty and staff members of all ranks, enabling community, learning, and scholarship (Cox, 2004; Beach & Cox, 2009). In addition to community and scholarship, group mentoring in faulty learning communities has been successful because of the multidisciplinarity of members and yearlong structure. Evidence shows that participation in faculty learning communities gets participants out of the silos of their disciplines and increases interest in teaching and in the scholarship of teaching and learning (Beach & Cox, 2009).

In an extensive study of 15 years of mentoring in our learning community for junior faculty at Miami University, we found interesting long-term patterns (Cox, 1997). For example, after 5 years, 25% of the mentors who served in a given year were former mentees and 25% were repeat mentors. As the program continued into a second decade, the number of repeat mentors in a given year increased to 40%. Once selecting more than one mentor was a possibility, each year one third of the junior faculty in the program selected two mentors. In the second decade of the program, this increased to 40%, with half of the mentees who choose two mentors selecting one from inside their departments and one from outside. Evidence also shows that Miami's early-career faculty in this faculty learning community program were tenured at a significantly higher rate than those who did not participate (Cox, 1995). This group mentoring program received the 1994 Hesburgh Award, given to the faculty development program judged best in the United States in fulfilling the three award criteria: significance of the program to higher education, appropriate program rationale, and successful results and impact on undergraduate teaching and learning.

At this point I recognize and acknowledge the excellent work of Robert Boice, a colleague who researched and provided valuable recommendations about mentoring (Boice, 1992a). His book and many of his articles on mentoring published during the 1990s inspired and guided me toward effective mentoring approaches while working with early-career academics. My favorite Boice (1992b) quote is, "Mentoring pairs need mentoring" (p. 55). Authors Phillips and Dennison acknowledge Boice's work and include many of his perspectives and recommendations in this volume.

I turn now to a perspective on mentoring not directly discussed in this book, namely the mentoring of students and faculty in transition and disequilibrium with respect to cognitive-structural intellectual development. The confusion and pain of students in such disequilibria can present the most pressing need for mentoring in higher education. On the threshold of transition, this disequilibrium can result in nagging student behaviors and statements such as, "Why do we have to do group work? It's such a waste of time! Just lecture and tell us what we need to know." There are other transition behaviors that call for mentoring; for example, why a student is reluctant to contribute to discussions or find his or her voice when writing, or why students struggle when there is no one correct answer and find it frustrating to determine how one answer is better than another. We see equivalent behaviors and hear similar statements from colleagues, such as, "Why should I use group work in my teaching? It's such a waste of my time! I just want to tell students what they need to know. That way I cover all the content."

To assist students and faculty in these situations, there are developmental schemes that mentors should learn about and engage, as Kloss (1994) notes:

> Much if not most of the bewildering student behavior I had been at a loss to understand fell into place on the scheme, and I then both understood them and judged them less harshly as a result. (p. 152)

In this foreword I do not have space to delve into much detail, but I shall provide glimpses and references. Phillips and Dennison provide the mentoring tools that can address such instances, but the concerns will vary by individual and situation. There is no mentoring procedure that fits all.

Of interest here is the view that learning involves structures, called "positions" or "stages," which are sets of assumptions individuals use in order to adapt to and organize their environments. Cognitive-structural theories examine the process of intellectual development, focusing on how a person thinks, reasons, and makes meaning of his or her experiences. These structures can change and become more complex as an individual experiences life in the college years and beyond. The stages arise one at a time and always in the same order regardless of cultural conditions. A person's age and the time that he or she spends in a stage are variables. Each stage incorporates aspects of and is more complex than the previous one (Evans et al., 1998).

Three evidenced-based theories describe structures that can inform mentors working with students and colleagues in disequilibria during the process of transition.

William Perry (1970, 1999), as director of Harvard's Bureau of Study Counsel, discovered patterns in student responses to the question, "What would you like to say has stood out for you during the year?" Perry called the structures "positions," and he identified nine, noting each as a resting place, with

development occurring during transition, a period of disequilibrium that could be eased by mentoring by the instructor and peer support. The nine positions are sometimes grouped into four descriptions. Perry called the first one *dualism,* in which learners have difficulty with ambiguity and see the instructor as authority and expert with the correct answers. Students who are dualists prefer lectures and do not value the opinions of peers, for example in group work. The second grouping of positions is *multiplicity,* where learners become comfortable with ambiguity and consider all opinions equally valuable, unable to judge the relative merits of different opinions. *Relativism,* the third descriptive area, finds students able to locate and cite evidence and use reasoning to determine and advocate for the opinion they choose to select. Most instructors want to move students to this position because it is a position for critical thinking. A learner in the fourth grouping, *commitment in relativism,* does not become different in terms of cognitive complexity, but rather employs relativism to make choices of personal value such as selection of major, career, relationships, and moral and ethical approaches.

Women's Ways of Knowing (Belenky, Clinchy, Goldberger, & Tarule, 1986) built upon Gilligan's (1982) work to expand Perry's (1970, 1999) approach. Gilligan moved the discourse of objective individualism to include relationship and the themes of care and justice. The learners interviewed by Belenky et al. included women of diverse ages, lives, and outlooks. Belenky et al. called their structures "perspectives"; found the development of voice, mind, and self to be intertwined; viewed the role of teacher as midwife; and were advocates of connected teaching, group learning, and trust in student work. They named their sequence of five structures silence, received knowing, subjective knowing, procedural knowing (connected or separate), and constructed knowing. Their second through fifth stages are parallel to the groupings of Perry's positions.

Marcia Baxter Magolda (1992) identified four structures and called them "stages." She discovered and included gender differences in her structures, which parallel those of Perry (1970, 1999) and Belenky et al. (1986). Baxter Magolda interviewed a cohort of 101 first-year undergraduate students beginning in 1986—a cohort she continues to follow in a longitudinal study that continues after graduation and through life experiences such as graduate school, careers, families, health issues, marriage, and divorce. Baxter Magolda (1992) states, "Understanding college students' intellectual development is at the heart of educational practice" (p. 3). In her longitudinal study Baxter Magolda (2001) discovered the difference between those who are successful at addressing change and challenge in adult life and those who struggle to do so. Those who were successful had developed contextual knowing (the fourth stage) during or soon after their college years.

Each of these three structural development theories has applications to mentoring. These approaches can address a course learning objective that involves connecting with where students are in their cognitive development process and the support needed to engage transition.

Knefelkamp created a process for mentors to operationalize Perry's theory using four variables for challenge and support (Perry, 1999). Each variable can be viewed on a continuum based on the degree of engagement as the course progresses. The variables for a course are (a) structure—high degree (for dualists) to low (for those in relativism); (b) diversity in two areas—quantity (number of perspectives) and quality (complexity of concepts, tasks); (c) experiential learning (degree of connecting to students' experiences such as service learning); and (d) personalism (degree of mentor and student support using community, interaction, listening, and safety to encourage risk taking).

Belenky et al. (1986) operationalize their model by using connected teaching: connecting students to students (cooperative learning groups, building classroom community), faculty to students (listening, discussion), students to families and the local and global community (oral histories, service learning, study abroad), and courses to courses (linked courses, team teaching).

Baxter Magolda and King (2004) recommend the use of learning partnerships to develop self-authorship. Kegan (1994) defines *self-authorship* as composing one's own reality by internally coordinating beliefs, values, and interpersonal loyalties rather than depending on external values, beliefs, and interpersonal loyalties. Baxter Magolda and King (2004) warn, "Substantial evidence suggests that self-authorship is uncommon during college. . . . Those who graduate from college without the internal foundation follow external formulas for adult life" (p. xxiii). "Relying on external authority allowed them to succeed in college but was insufficient for life after graduation" (p. 28). Learning partnerships engage learners through challenge and support to develop cognitive maturity, integrated identity, and mature relationships. Building this foundation with a mentor aware of these dynamics can be the most important learning partnership in higher education.

With this call to mentoring though groups, learning communities, personalism, and learning partnerships, I encourage your reading of this book to find, among its wealth of perspectives, the approach that works best for you, your students, and your colleagues.

Milton D. Cox
Director, Original Lilly Conference on College Teaching; and Editor-in-Chief, *Journal on Excellence in College Teaching* and *Learning Communities Journal*, Miami University
June 11, 2014

References

Baxter Magolda, M. (1992). *Knowing and reasoning in college: Gender-related patterns in students' intellectual development.* San Francisco: Jossey-Bass.

Baxter Magolda, M. (2001). *Making their own way: Narratives for transforming higher education to promote self-development.* Sterling, VA: Stylus.

Baxter Magolda, M. & King, P. M. (Eds.). (2004). *Learning partnerships: Theory and models of practice to educate for self-authorship.* Sterling, VA: Stylus.

Beach, A. L. & Cox, M. D. (2009). The impact of faculty learning communities on teaching and learning. *Learning Communities Journal, 1*(1), 7–27

Belenky, M. B., Clinchy, B. M., Goldberger, N. R., & Tarule, J. M. (1986). *Women's ways of knowing: The development of self, voice, and mind.* New York: Basic Books.

Boice, R. (1992a). *The new faculty member: Supporting and fostering professional development.* San Francisco: Jossey-Bass.

Boice, R. (1992b). Lessons learned about mentoring. *New Directions for Teaching and Learning, (1992)*51, 51–61.

Boyer, E. L. (1990). *Scholarship reconsidered: Priorities of the professoriate.* Princeton, NJ: The Carnegie Foundation for the Advancement of Teaching.

Cox, M. D. (Fall, 1977). How to design and implement a Pi Mu Epsilon conference. *The Pi Mu Epsilon Journal, (6)*7, 400–402.

Cox, M. D. (1995). The development of new and junior faculty. In W. A. Wright and Associates (Eds.), *Teaching improvement practices: Successful strategies for higher education* (pp. 283–310). Bolton, MA: Anker.

Cox, M. D. (1997). Long-term patterns in a mentoring program for junior faculty: Recommendations for practice. In D. Dezure (Ed.), *To Improve the Academy: Vol. 16. Resources for faculty, instructional, and organizational development* (pp. 225–268). Stillwater, OK: New Forums Press.

Cox, M. D. (2003). Fostering the scholarship of teaching through faculty learning communities. *Journal on Excellence in College Teaching, 14*(2/3), 161–198.

Cox, M. D. (2004). Introduction to faculty learning communities. *New Directions for Teaching and Learning, (2004)*97, 5–23.

Cox, M. D. (2009). Connecting faculty and student learning communities: Challenges, successes, and recommendations. *Learning Communities Journal, 1*(2), 19–47.

Gilligan, C. (1982). *In a different voice: Psychological theory and women's development.* Cambridge, MA: Harvard University Press.

Evans, N. J., Forney, D. S., & Guido-DiBrito, F. (1998). *Student development in college: Theory, research, and practice.* San Francisco: Jossey-Bass.

Johnson, D. W., Johnson, R. T., & Smith, K. A. (1998). *Active learning: Cooperation in the college classroom.* Edina, MN: Interaction.

Kegan, R. (1994). *In over our heads: The mental demands of modern life.* Cambridge, MA: Harvard University Press.

Kloss, R. (1994). A nudge is best: Helping students through the Perry scheme of intellectual development, *College Teaching, 42*(4), 151–158.

Perry, W. J. (1970). *Forms of intellectual and ethical development in the college years.* New York: Holt, Rinehart, and Winston.

Perry, W. J. (1999). *Forms of intellectual and ethical development in the college years.* San Francisco: Jossey-Bass.

Acknowledgments

We would like to thank those who helped our writing process by graciously agreeing to be interviewed in their various roles regarding mentoring. The section in chapter 2 on advice to new mentors was informed by interviews with Dr. Heidi Carlone, Associate Professor of Education; Dr. Kathy Jamieson, Associate Professor of Kinesiology; Dr. Christian Moraru, Professor of English; and Dr. Jonathan Tudge, Professor of Human Development and Family Studies. Department chairs who were helpful in defining the issues addressed in chapter 5 were Dr. Christopher Poulos, Communication Studies; Dr. Gavin Douglas, Music Education; Ms. Mary Krautter, Library; and Dr. Patricia Crane, Nursing. Provost David Perrin and Dean Timothy Johnston offered insights into mentoring from an administrator's perspective for chapter 6. Dr. Bonnie Canzioni, Professor of Hospitality Management, provided great help to us regarding assessment procedures. We would also like to thank Dr. Milton D. Cox, author of the foreword; as well as all those who have participated in the UNCG New Faculty Mentoring Program over the years, and from whom we have learned so much.

Susan L. Phillips
Susan T. Dennison

Introduction:
Overview and Purpose of the Manual

Higher education settings today face the challenge of providing a new generation of students with knowledge and skills for a much more competitive and globally minded world. At the same time, universities are dealing with some of the most economically difficult times as their budgets are repeatedly cut. So how are these institutions going to provide a quality education to the same number of, or even more, students during these particularly demanding times? One answer is to make the recruitment and retention of a vibrant, bright, and diverse faculty a clear priority. And one of the key ways to attain this last objective is through well-planned, formalized faculty mentoring programs. The purpose of faculty mentoring is to develop an academic atmosphere that mutually nurtures, supports, and further develops all faculty members' teaching and research skills and assists them so that they feel part of a university/college community.

This manual provides timely, important, and relevant material on setting up, conducting, and assessing a new faculty mentoring program, regardless of whether it is one-on-one, group, or a combination of both formats. A cross-section of a university faculty members and administrators, including new faculty members on tenure-track positions and those on term appointments (e.g., clinical faculty members, adjuncts), minority faculty and international faculty, senior faculty serving as mentors, department chairs/heads, faculty development center staff, deans, and provosts, will find specific sections of this manual pertinent to

their roles in a faculty mentoring program. We offer a user-friendly format throughout this text in that guidelines are listed concisely and clearly so everyone involved in faculty mentoring can quickly apply and/or modify the material to meet his or her specific needs.

Although formalized mentoring addresses the needs of universities, the main focus is support of new faculty members. The most common concerns among new faculty arc a sense of isolation and lack of support or respect during their pre-tenure years. Many feel that they are in a sink-or-swim situation with few resources. A well-thought-out program lets new faculty know that the university cares about them and their success.

Universities without a campus-wide formal mentoring program find that mentoring efforts on campus are often uneven, with some departments providing excellent mentoring and some providing none. Perceptions of the effectiveness of mentoring can vary widely between faculty and administration. This manual provides you with methods for supporting departmental mentoring as well as establishing school-/college- or university-wide mentoring programs.

Approaching mentoring in an intentional way can address many issues facing higher education today. Recruitment and retention of a diverse faculty is one such issue. The national average age of faculty is 54 years, with an average retirement age of 62.5 years (Conley, 2007) and a wave of retirements expected in the next 10 years. With impending retirements and a national shortage of faculty in some disciplines, competition for faculty hires will be increasing. Retention (along with recruitment) has been found to be a key element for increasing minority and ethnic faculty representation, and mentoring has been found to be especially beneficial in this regard (Boice, 1992; Brinson & Kottler, 1993; de Janasz & Sullivan, 2004). National figures put the tenure rate for minority faculty at two-thirds that for White faculty (Brinson & Kottler, 1993).

A second issue is financial. Institutions of higher education have always needed to be mindful of cost containment, and mentoring programs can address issues involved in the cost of hiring new faculty. Recruitment and hiring of faculty is an expensive process. The estimated cost of hiring a new faculty member (including advertising, travel for interviews, hotels and meals, and time spent by the search committee and staff) is equal to a year's salary for the new hire (Detmar, 2004). The average direct cost of recruiting and interviewing for a school within our university was $7,000 per hire. The indirect costs of staff and faculty time in the search and hiring process are at least $18,000. Start-up costs for research support ranged from $40,000 to $100,000. Increased retention, therefore, results in reduced costs associated with hiring. Considering the costliness of making a new hire, it makes good business sense to maximize support for the success of new faculty in whom we have invested so much already.

Given the many benefits that faculty mentoring programs can offer higher education institutions today, this manual provides the necessary details involved in setting up, planning, conducting, and evaluating faculty mentoring programs both within a department setting and at the university-/college-wide level. After reading this manual, you will be able to replicate either the example faculty mentoring program delineated in chapter 6 or the one-on-one mentoring presented in chapter 1 for mentors. However, you can read the material in every chapter quickly and use it to meet the needs of new faculty, including adjuncts and those on or off the tenure track, as well as senior faculty, including those who serve as department heads or mentors, and higher education administrators, as each chapter stands alone in advice and guidelines to

each of these groups. The example faculty mentoring program outlined in chapter 6 is well grounded in the current literature and studies summarized in chapter 7. Examples of other models are also provided in this chapter, as is a discussion of funding and sustainability issues. Each chapter addresses strategies for monitoring and assessment.

This book addresses everyone involved in the mentoring process. It provides guidance to mentors on how to start, conduct, and conclude a mentoring relationship, and on the characteristics needed to establish a good relationship with mentees. It offers mentees advice on what to expect, selecting mentors for specific purposes, and when to seek mentors outside their departments. For department chairs, deans, provosts, and directors of faculty development centers, it describes the range and type of mentoring arrangements, whether one-on-one, group-based, or organized at the department or institutional level, and offers templates for setting up and assessing them, as well as information on cost/benefits. The audience intended to benefit from this practical guide is intentionally very wide. Obviously, senior faculty mentors, along with new faculty mentees, will find this manual most useful. But, in addition, university/ college administrators (i.e., provosts and deans) will find that the material in this book can be replicated and modified easily to meet their university/college setting's needs. Thus, this user-friendly feature of the manual also addresses the realities of today's higher education economic challenges. Moreover, department heads/chairs will find much of this manual useful as they match junior faculty members with senior faculty mentors. It also provides guidance on how to maximize benefits from these mentoring relationships. Appendices B through I present worksheets and forms that you can adapt to your program's needs (also available for free download at www.Styluspub.com).

Chapter 1, which is addressed to mentors, focuses on the one-on-one mentoring relationship, whether it is conducted within a new faculty member's department or through a university-wide program. Mentors will learn which of their qualities contribute to an effective mentoring relationship with a new faculty member. We have provided guidelines for the ideal frequency of mentoring sessions, potential questions to ask a new mentee, how to best structure these one-on-one sessions, and strategies for eliciting ongoing assessment from a new faculty member. Senior faculty mentors will find suggestions for meeting the needs most frequently reported by new faculty members. In particular, faculty mentors will learn a wide variety of strategies for exploring issues, such as establishing a satisfying work/life balance, how to stay focused on one's research and writing, and how to improve one's teaching without spending enormous amounts of time on overpreparation.

Chapter 2 offers guidelines for setting up, planning, and conducting group mentoring. The introductory material on group work in this section includes the unique benefits new faculty acquire from this mentoring format. Details regarding the best ways to compose these groups are also delineated in this chapter. We also discuss the importance and specific use of contracting for commitment and confidentiality with group members, along with the rationale for using such formal commitments. A standard format for group sessions is outlined, along with the purpose of each component of this routine. We also provide planning guidelines in this chapter, with examples of related task sheets contained in appendices B, C, and D. In addition, we list specific guidelines for facilitating these groups, along with ways that facilitation changes as a mentoring group develops.

Chapter 3 focuses on how junior faculty members can maximize the potential benefits of a mentoring relationship. We identify guidelines for selecting an ideal senior faculty mentor, along with the advantages of having a mentor within and outside one's department, including mentors for different aspects of one's academic life. New faculty members will learn which of their most common needs a senior faculty mentor typically addresses. Self-rating questionnaires are also provided to help new faculty members articulate more clearly what they specifically need from their mentor in Appendix G.

Chapter 4 offers guidelines to department chairs/heads on how to set up and support faculty mentoring within their department. This section of the book will show the reader how to easily and quickly modify related material in Appendix H so they can set up and maintain a departmental faculty mentoring program. This section also provides guidance on matching up new faculty members to senior faculty mentors and outlines the benefits the latter can derive from such a relationship. In addition, we reference relevant task sheets for department heads in chapter 4 that are provided in Appendix H. Finally, we include a system for monitoring and assessing the efficacy of these one-on-one mentoring relationships.

Chapter 5 offers material about setting up and supporting faculty mentoring programs for university/college provosts, deans, and directors of faculty development. We explain practical guidelines for establishing and maintaining a faculty mentoring program and offer a model that can easily be adapted or modified to suit individual institutional missions. Furthermore, we address the typical financial costs of running such programs and discuss the corresponding costs and benefits/savings such a resource can achieve for new faculty members. Also, this chapter provides some critical material on how administrators can evaluate and monitor these faculty mentoring programs so that they are continuously improved. In addition, guidelines for modifying this material are also provided so university/college administrators have strategies for developing similar programs that better fit within their budgets and meet the individual needs of their institution.

Chapter 6 addresses the director of a faculty mentoring program that combines individual and group mentoring. The chapter begins with proposal development, piloting the program, and planning for assessment. This is followed by detailed implementation instructions, with a model program as an example. The details include recruitment of mentors and mentees, opening activities, monthly program and monitoring, and closing activities.

Chapter 7 reviews the literature on which this manual is grounded, covering such issues as the importance of faculty mentoring programs, the typical logistics involved, benefits reported by new faculty members, value of these relationships for senior faculty mentors, challenges involved in these programs, strategies for effectively evaluating the efficacy of these relationships, and issues of sustainability of these programs.

The appendices provide task sheets and other materials referenced in chapters 1 through 6 that will make replication of the suggestions for mentoring on either a one-on-one or in groups much easier to accomplish. In addition, Appendix A offers a topical bibliography, including books and a table of websites on faculty mentoring programs. The references are arranged by topic area for ease of locating resources for a specific need.

References

Boice, R. (1992). *The new faculty member: Supporting and fostering professional development*. San Francisco: Jossey-Bass.

Brinson, J., & Kottler, J. (1993). Cross-cultural mentoring in counselor education: A strategy for retaining minority faculty. *Counselor Education and Supervision, 32*(4), 241–253.

Conley, V. (2007). Retirement and benefits: Expectations and realities. *The NEA 2007 Almanac of Higher Education*. Washington, DC: National Education Association.

de Jansaz, S., & Sullivan, S. (2004). Multiple mentoring in the academe: Developing the professional network. *Journal of Vocational Behavior, 64*, 263–285.

Detmar, K. (2004). What we waste when faculty hiring goes wrong. *The Chronicle of Higher Education, 51*(17), 86–88.

CHAPTER 1

Tips for Mentors Inside or Outside the Department

"Our meetings allowed me to decompress, gain an alternate perspective on my lived experiences, and learn from a senior scholar."

—Mentee comment

When we ask experienced mentors about the characteristics of good mentors, we receive similar responses. The first attributes to come to mind are openness and a willingness to share. Mentoring is exciting in the same way that research is exciting: We can be open to new discoveries. A good mentor is able to see things from multiple perspectives, and each mentee brings new expertise and experience to the relationship. None will have the same experience you had as a new faculty member, though there may be similarities. The life of the academy has changed a lot for new faculty members. Although you bring years of experience to your role as mentor, you must also have the humility to acknowledge what you don't know. This aspect of openness brings a sense of humanity to the relationship in the increasingly corporate atmosphere of today's universities. The most important part of openness is to be a good listener. Although new faculty members appreciate the advice they receive from their mentors, they overwhelmingly report that the most important aspect of the relationship is that someone actually cares about them and their success.

The second characteristic experienced mentors delineate is trust. The sense of support and encouragement that new faculty members derive from the mentoring relationship relies on two aspects of trust.

The first is a mutual respect between members of the mentoring dyad. This must be a collaborative relationship, not something imposed from the top down. This mutual respect can be particularly important to a very new professor who may still be feeling the effects of the "imposter syndrome," or the sense that one is not really qualified for the position. A belief in one's credentials and expertise can go a long way in the development of a new faculty member's fragile competence. The second is the creation of a safe space within the relationship. Don't be shy about sharing your own experiences as an untenured faculty member. It is helpful to hear that someone else has experienced difficulties on the road to tenure and survived them. Part of this sense of safety comes from strict confidentiality and protection of the mentee's privacy. This can be a tricky component when mentoring within the department as it is important for the department head to monitor and assess the efficacy of the relationship, and this must be done without putting that sense of safety at risk. The fact that an in-department mentor will vote on the mentee's tenure also introduces a power component to the relationship, which may result in the mentee being less forthcoming about his or her concerns and worries. For this reason, we recommend that the mentee have a second mentor outside the department (see Sidebar 1.1).

SIDEBAR 1.1

Areas in which a mentor can actively help

- Reading manuscripts, monographs, chapters
- Watching presentations
- Reading grant proposals
- Long- and short-term goal planning
- Writing a teaching philosophy
- Writing a research narrative
- Preparing a portfolio/dossier
- Formative assessment of teaching
- Making connections on and off campus
- Advice on negotiations with department head
- Advice on how to use a graduate assistant
- Advice on student difficulties

A third characteristic of good mentors is the ability to see things in a holistic way. It is important to work with the totality of the life of the new professor. There are ways to help a new professor efficiently prepare for teaching, plan a research agenda, and strategize about service commitments while maintaining work-life balance to avoid burnout. Another aspect of holistic mentoring is the ability to see the big picture from the smaller concerns the mentee describes. In other words, what is this story really about?

What Do You Have to Offer?

If you are new to mentoring, take some time to list your personal strengths and to consider what style of mentoring might best suit your personality. Let us suggest several potential strengths that you bring to the relationship, based on comments from both mentees and mentors.

- You know the culture of the department and institution. This may seem like a given, but mentees appreciate that knowledge base. It also provides a continuity that is meaningful to department heads and other administrators.

- You have been where they are. This provides you with strong empathy that cannot be found in an outside life coach.
- You have the ability to reframe an issue in a larger context. A simple example is the one nasty comment in a semester-end course evaluation.
- You have experience with goal setting and prioritizing university commitments.
- You understand the tenure experience and, perhaps, the tenure criteria. An out-of-department mentor will have to be clear about this and offer helpful suggestions to the mentee for determining departmental criteria.
- You have experience with college students at your institution; they may be very different from those where the new professor may have taught as a graduate teaching assistant.
- You have experience with the annual review process. Again, this may vary between departments or schools and the outside mentor should be aware of this.

What Are the Characteristics of New Faculty Members?

Boice (1992) outlined five characteristics that we find to be true today. New faculty members (a) overprepare for teaching and (b) teach defensively. Consequently they (c) spend less time than necessary on scholarly writing. Nevertheless, they (d) tend to perform on the lower end in course evaluations. And amid all of these stressful experiences, they (e) feel isolated, experiencing loneliness and frustration. To these we would add that mentees on our campus recognize the imposter syndrome in themselves when it is described to them. Initially, some of them may not fully grasp the difference between being a successful graduate student and a successful faculty member. The duties and expectations of full faculty members are not taught in most graduate programs.

Boice (1992) also noted the characteristics of quick starters, which we describe here so you can encourage them in your mentees.

- They develop work habits to reflect their goals.
- They write multiple times per week.

- They connect with faculty across campus.
- They prepare adequately for engaged teaching.
- They integrate teaching and research.
- They strategically plan service obligations.
- They seek mentoring.

What Do New Faculty Members Need?

Our experience suggests that there are areas in which faculty from all disciplines need guidance.

- They need to feel connected with others and the larger community.
- They need help with time management.
- They need help with prioritizing.
- They need advice with balancing teaching and research.
- They need advice with balancing work and life outside the university.
- They need editorial help with their writing (particularly if English is their second language).

Potential Questions You Can Ask Your Mentee

Following are lists of questions from which you can choose, depending upon the needs of your mentee, whether you are an in-department or outside mentor, and upon your style of mentoring. Asking questions is an excellent form of guidance and avoids the possibility that you will project your experiences onto your mentee.

Questions Concerning Departmental Expectations for Tenure

- Do you know what your departmental expectations are and/or where to find them (in writing)?
- Do you have a sense of senior faculty expectations?
- Do you have a five-year plan?
- What are the most important requirements for tenure? Is there debate about this in the department?

- What type of authorship is expected?
- What is within your control?

Overarching Questions

- Why do you choose to do your work in the academy?
- What do you feel your contribution to your field will be?
- How is your fit within the department?
- How do you find community in your work (inside or outside your university)?
- What is your trajectory?
- What is your projected image of professionalism?

Questions for Regular Meetings

- How was your week/month?
- What are you working on right now?
- How are you managing your goals?
- How is your writing coming along?
- Any new possibilities for funding?
- What do you need/how can I help?

Stages of the Mentoring Relationship

Opening Stage: Set the Parameters

- Get to know your mentee. Consider using some of the questions listed above. In addition, relationship-building activities can be found in Appendix B.
- Talk about expectations for the relationship and set limits. When limits are clear, your mentee will be more likely to feel comfortable about seeking your guidance.
- The mentor makes first contact. Most junior faculty are loathe to ask senior faculty for help or advice simply because they see them as too busy. Within the department this is also due to a reluctance to seem less than competent.
- Define goals (needs assessment checklist). These can include goals for the relationship,

particularly if there is a defined time span for the relationship, as well as long-term and short-term career goals. Needs may vary, depending upon whether the mentee is tenure-track, nontenure-track, or adjunct faculty.

- Discuss confidentiality; this is particularly important for an interdepartmental relationship.

Second Stage: Regular Meetings

- Define the length of the relationship. Consider the possibility that the formal relationship might be only one year. Although the relationship can certainly continue on an informal basis afterward, a regular change in mentor provides new excitement, interest, and viewpoints. A lengthy relationship can become stale and unproductive, and unduly burdensome for the mentor.

- Define the schedule of meetings, which should take place no less frequently than once a month. It may be that for a first-year faculty member, meetings will occur more frequently for the first month or two.

- Discuss where you would like to meet. We suggest informal meetings over coffee or walks on campus, though some prefer a more formal meeting in the mentor's office. Meetings over meals are not as productive, as there are interruptions for ordering and much time is spent eating.

- Discuss attending events together. This is a nice way to introduce a mentee to others across campus and make event attendance more comfortable for a new faculty member.

- Discuss the possibility of a formative assessment of teaching, and whether this would involve one observation, mutual observations of teaching, or multiple observations of the mentee's teaching.

- Do an informal midyear evaluation. One possibility is a modification of a midterm course evaluation. Have the mentee complete the following statements: "Please start . . . ." "There is no need to continue . . . ." "Please continue . . . ."

Third Stage: Evolution Into a Collegial Relationship

- Expect needs to decrease over time. Although your mentee may feel more secure in his or her position and in the knowledge that you are there if something comes up, the second semester is a good time to look at things like annual reports and negotiating next year's workload. We provide closure tasks in Appendix D.

- Connections become infrequent. After the relationship is established in the first semester, you might ask that the mentee set up future meetings. Don't be surprised if these don't happen as frequently.

- Discuss finding new mentor(s). Does your mentee have someone else he or she would like to work with? What qualities is your mentee looking for? Perhaps the next mentor would be someone who can help the mentee with a particular project.

- Assess the efficacy of the relationship in a formative manner. If you are doing interdepartmental mentoring, your department head may require a more summative assessment. A university-wide program will mandate an end-of-year evaluation for both mentors and mentees.

- Become colleagues. Although the formal relationship may last only one year, an informal relationship will continue in many cases, even if the mentee is not in your department. One mentor in our acquaintance formed a writing accountability group with mentees and former mentees, but simply attending events together or having coffee together once or twice a year is more typical.

Interdepartmental Versus Intradepartmental Mentoring

These two mentoring roles are similar in many ways, but different in focus. An external mentor will be able to address many of the issues of new faculty members, but will not have knowledge of their areas of research. For new faculty members, the most important benefit of an outside mentor is having someone to talk with about their concerns who will not be voting on their tenure. It is natural that junior faculty will not want to express their worries to departmental colleagues. In general, however, an outside mentor can ask all of the questions in the previous section and provide a great deal of guidance that, due to the external circumstances, must encourage self-sufficiency in the mentee to answer those questions.

In some ways, mentoring a new colleague inside your department is more difficult than mentoring one outside your department. Colleagues within a department may be in competition for limited resources. If a mentee makes what seems to you to be an unreasonable demand, an outside mentor can ask, "What is the culture in your department regarding expectations about that?" without the potential for being affected personally. The interdepartmental mentor will know the history of the department but may need to find a tactful way to communicate the history and culture of the department to the mentee.

It can be difficult to juggle the collegial and mentoring relationships. There is a danger that the relationship could be seen as surveillance, resulting in the mentee avoiding certain topics about which he or she could use some advice. The mentor, after all, will be participating in the tenure decision about the mentee. This introduces a power differential into the relationship that cannot be circumvented. If an outside mentor can be established, then each mentoring dyad can be clear about the purpose of its respective relationship.

Advice From Mentors

This section offers advice for those new to mentoring, straight from the mouths of experienced mentors.

You need a good match to be effective. A good match can mean many things. The first mentors, whether inside or outside the department, are most effective if the personalities involved "click." They also work best if the relationship is mutually agreed upon,

rather than being assigned. Once the mentee is more established, the choice of mentor may be based on expertise.

There is more than one way to mentor effectively, and it changes with each new person. You must mentor from who you are. This advice is similar to Parker Palmer's advice about teaching from who you are (Palmer, 1998). This follows naturally from the idea that a good match is important. Everyone has a style of mentoring, and no one mentor can fill all the needs of a mentee. You also have to work with the personality of your mentee; we find that most new faculty fall into two general categories. Some will want your time together to relax from their stressful lives. Others will feel the need to be constantly "on task," concerned that they do not waste one minute of productive time. You may see the need for those in the first category to use you to hold their feet to the fire, and for those in the latter to make sure they include de-stressing activities in their schedule.

Make time to reflect on the process and prepare for meetings. Set aside time in your schedule each week; think about it outside the monthly meetings; and consider what questions you want to ask and what worksheets (found in appendices C and H) you might want to use. In addition, read articles about mentoring or other topics that might be helpful to your mentee. The time commitment is crucial; it isn't just volunteerism.

Don't try to fix things; just understand them. This can be difficult, as most of us are natural problem solvers. There is an urge to smooth things over, but it is okay to be frustrated.

Be willing to tell your mentee what he or she should not be doing, including new "opportunities" that may sidetrack the mentee. One method might be to delineate goals, then what supports are available to achieve them, and what distractions or roadblocks there are to attaining them. In some cases, encouragement to find ways to say no will be welcomed, and your mentee may need some ideas for how to do this in a positive way. If a mentee's department head also wishes to protect his or her time, then an agreement can be made that all requests for service must be run through the department head. Saying no to colleagues in the department can be more difficult, and here is where actually having writing time scheduled into your calendar can allow the mentee to say, "I'm so sorry; I already have something scheduled at that time."

It is even more difficult for a mentor to recognize that something the mentee thinks is a great opportunity is actually not in his or her best interest, usually because it is time-consuming and will not further the mentee's quest for tenure. One method of dealing with this scenario is to ask questions of the mentee: How much time will be involved? Where will you document this in your tenure portfolio?

Make sure there is recognition for mentoring in your department. Mentoring should count for service to the department, school, or university, depending upon whom you are mentoring. If you are mentoring outside your department, ask for a letter of thanks and recognition of your time and effort that is copied to your department head in time for annual review.

Seek peer mentoring for yourself. There are two ways to go about this. One is to find a colleague outside your department, ideally someone who is also mentoring or has done so. Another is to form a small group of senior faculty involved in mentoring. It is very helpful to run issues by colleagues to benefit from the collective wisdom in the room. It is also rejuvenating to discuss the life of academia and the well-being of junior faculty in a community of like-minded colleagues. Mentors feel that it provides a community-wide scholarly space.

Rewards to the Mentor

Mentors report many personal benefits. One is that by thinking about negotiating an academic career, you learn about yourself in a more holistic way. It gives you time to reflect on your own life as an academic. Mentoring outside your department also gives you a broader perspective on the university community because you learn about how things are done in other departments. Last, mentors say that it makes them better departmental colleagues. They are more aware of protecting junior colleagues, whether or not they may be formally mentoring that person. As one mentor put it, "The work itself is the reward. It adds a piece to my work that would otherwise not be there."

References

Boice, R. (1992). *The new faculty member: Supporting and fostering professional development.* San Francisco: Jossey-Bass.

Palmer, P. J. (1998). *The courage to teach: Exploring the inner landscape of a teacher's life.* San Francisco: Jossey-Bass.

CHAPTER 2

Guidelines for Setting Up, Planning, and Facilitating a Mentoring Group

"Having contact with people outside your department keeps you sane. Otherwise, I would have no one to talk to about some major issues."

—Mentee comment

The primary purpose of this chapter is to provide step-by-step guidelines for setting up, planning, and facilitating mentoring groups for new faculty members. These groups have been called Learning Communities during the first five years of the New Faculty Mentoring Program at The University of North Carolina at Greensboro (UNCG). These groups are similar to what Cox (1999) terms *cohort-focused faculty learning communities*, but they have been expanded to address more than junior faculty members' teaching. Rather, these mentoring groups address any of the many challenges or concerns new faculty members face as they begin their career at a university or college.

Before providing guidelines for planning and facilitating mentoring groups, we delineate the Dennison Group Practice model (Dennison, 1989), which provides the rationale for the guidelines in this chapter. In addition, this group practice model will help senior faculty facilitators understand, in greater depth, how mentoring groups are different from individual mentoring and some of the unique benefits of these groups.

Faculty members who have not been trained formally in group work are strongly advised to review this practice model before reviewing the guidelines for setting up, planning, and facilitating these mentoring groups. Even experienced group facilitators should take the time to understand this approach to mentoring groups because it is somewhat different from some more traditional practice models on group work. One of the unique features of this group practice model's development has been its refinement specifically for faculty mentoring groups. During the last five years we have systematically collected qualitative data from focus groups with new faculty mentoring groups at our university.

Dennison Group Practice Model

The initial development of the Dennison Group Practice model was based on Yalom's (1985) work with the therapeutic factors of group psychotheraphy. However, much of this model's later development has been informed by our experience working with specific groups, as in this case new faculty mentoring groups. Table 2.1 shows how groups are viewed, following this group model, as going through the three phases of initial, middle, and termination. In addition, two sets of goals, process goals and targeted group goals, for each phase are delineated on the same table, along with a guide indicating which goals are primary and which are secondary in each phase. The process goals of a mentoring group are essentially the same for all groups since attaining these goals creates an attractive or appealing group setting, engages all participants in discussions and sharing, and begins to build a supportive and trusting community among the membership. In contrast, the targeted group goals are those goals specific to each faculty mentoring group since these goals focus on the problems or concerns common to a particular group. These primary and secondary goals and the related guide are particularly helpful in planning and facilitating faculty mentoring groups.

A timing guide is also provided in Table 2.1 toward the bottom of each group phase showing approximately how many sessions the average faculty mentoring group takes to get through that phase. Last, the primary focus for each of the three phases is provided in the second to last row of each phase column. Facilitators of faculty mentoring groups are urged to refer to Table 2.1 as they review the following key application points of this model that are particularly relevant to new faculty mentoring groups.

TABLE 2.1
Dennison Group Practice Model: A Framework for a Faculty Mentoring Group

	Initial Phase	*Middle Phase*	*Termination Phase*
Primary Emphasis	Process Goals 1. To create an attractive or appealing and comfortable group for faculty members 2. To initiate balanced participation among the membership 3. To initiate relationship building among membership	Targeted Group Goals 1. To have members delineate in more detail their common areas of concern 2. To have members help one another problem solve their areas of concern 3. To provide instruction/resource identification in regard to members' areas of concern	Process Goals 1. To have members acknowledge the value of the group 2. To have members acknowledge what they have gained from the group 3. To have members identify other supports outside the group that will help them maintain their positive changes
Secondary Emphasis	Targeted Group Goals 1. To have members determine which aspects of their positions are most challenging 2. To have members prioritize which concerns in regard to their positions they want to currently address 3. To determine common areas of concern about one's position that members want to address	Process Goals 1. To maintain an attractive or appealing and comfortable group for faculty members 2. To maintain balanced participation among the membership 3. To increase bonding among members for group cohesiveness	Targeted Group Goals 1. To have members delineate their positive changes as a result of the group 2. To have members identify ways they will be able to maintain their positive changes 3. To have members acknowledge how the group has benefitted the entire membership
Primary Focus of Sessions	To bond the group's members and have them identify common areas of concern that the group can focus on in future sessions	To have members problem solve common areas of concern (targeted group goals)	To have members acknowledge value of group (process goals) and positive changes attained (targeted group goals)
Timing	4 to 6 sessions (first semester of group)	4 to 6 sessions (second semester of group)	Last session or maybe last two sessions

By Following the Dennison Group Practice Model Framework, These New Faculty Mentoring Groups Are Seen as Going Through Three Phases—Initial, Middle, and Termination

As seen in Table 2.1, a faculty mentoring group goes through three phases during the usual course of an academic year. In the fall semester these groups begin in the initial phase (far left column of Table 2.1), during which the facilitators plan ways to ensure that the group is attractive or appealing to the new faculty members, that all the members are willing to participate equally in each session, and that members begin building increasingly deeper relationships with one another. This is also the time in these groups when the membership needs to have tasks where they identify their current concerns about their faculty position, how they will prioritize these concerns, and which of these concerns are common among the group. Discussion of needs common to a group sets the stage for what particular aspects of the faculty members' positions the remaining sessions of a faculty mentoring group will focus on. These are what are termed in the Dennison Group Practice model as the *targeted group goals* and can include things like members learning more effective ways to be productive with their writing or increasing their skills for securing internal or external funding.

Typically faculty mentoring groups spend about four to six sessions in this initial phase, or what might coordinate with the fall semester in the academic year. As noted in Table 2.1, the process goals are primary in this phase because attaining these goals will provide members important benefits from participating in these groups as opposed to what they gain from one-on-one mentoring relationships. Frequently, faculty members in the UNCG Learning Communities Groups reported that some of the most important benefits from these groups included not feeling so alone as a new faculty member, realizing that other group members shared some of the challenges they were experiencing, and feeling for the first time that they had a safe and supportive group on campus.

The middle phase, the middle column in Table 2.1, is the working phase of these faculty mentoring groups. Typically groups are in this phase during most

of the spring semester. By this time, members are feeling fairly comfortable in the group and have established relationships with one another so that the group is bonded, or what is sometimes termed *cohesive*. In other words, members' relationships with one another help them to be potent motivators to both help one another make positive changes and stop behaviors that are not helping them in their faculty roles. This is the time when the membership should be most active in helping one another resolve concerns or problems they are having in meeting all the expectations in their faculty position. Typically facilitators should find that their planning of sessions is less time-consuming and their membership needs very little guidance in terms of conducting sessions.

The termination phase of the group (far right-hand column on Table 2.1) typically is only the last session of the group, and it is important that facilitators now shift the focus of the group to the ending process and targeted group goals. During this session members should share what positive changes they have made as a result of the group, what the value of the group has been for them, and how they can continue to maintain some of the positive changes they have made. Remember that it is incredibly valuable for members to make these acknowledgments to one another to reinforce both what they have gained from the group and the importance of this experience.

Every Group Should Address Two Sets of Goals, With One Set Being the Process Goals and the Second Set Being the Targeted Goals for a Group

Process goals are those goals that remain the same for any group, but what varies are the ways in which these goals are attained. The process goals focus on those aspects of the group that make it a unique and beneficial format for bonding group members and helping them to achieve their individual goals. As seen in Table 2.1, these goals are directed primarily at building a trusting and cohesive group, eliciting balanced participation from all members, and ensuring that the group remains attractive or appealing to its members. The second set of goals includes those specific targeted goals identified for each group. So in the case of faculty mentoring groups, each group would determine these goals, which would typically include members increasing their production of publications, securing external and internal funding, establishing important collegial relationships within one's department, and so on.

The Two Sets of Goals for a Group Vary in Their Emphasis During Each Phase of the Group

It is important for facilitators to note in Table 2.1 that a primary and secondary emphasis guide is provided for each group phase. As can be seen in this section of the table, process goals are of primary emphasis

in the initial and termination phases, while targeted group goals are of primary emphasis only in the middle phase. So why is this part of the Dennison Group Practice model important? This particular guide actually helps facilitators make a more direct connection between the goals for each phase and the resulting planning and facilitating of sessions. For example, group facilitators should refer to Tables 2.2 and 2.3, which contain specific guidelines for facilitators to set up, plan, and conduct their group sessions during each of the three phases.

TABLE 2.2
Suggestions for Attaining the Process Goals of a Faculty Mentoring Group

Phase of Group	*Process Goal*	*Suggestions for Attainment*
Initial	To create an attractive or appealing and comfortable group for faculty members	Provide refreshments Schedule at time that is good for all Hold meeting in comfortable setting Ensure facilitators are warm, honest, genuine, and open
	To initiate balanced participation among membership	Make sure everyone participates in tasks Plan relationship-building tasks that request the same disclosure of all members Talk outside group to members who talk too much or too little in group
	To initiate relationship building among membership	Start each session with relationship-building tasks Request factual and/or positive disclosure from members Participate in relationship-building tasks by modeling initially
Middle	To maintain an attractive or appealing and comfortable group for faculty members To maintain balanced participation among the membership To increase bonding among members for group cohesiveness	Maintain consistent attendance by all members Monitor that participation continues to be fairly balanced Do check-in exercise at onset of each session and consider changing session plan depending on what arises Have group recognize at the end of each session what was helpful/enjoyable
Termination	To have members acknowledge the value of the group To have members acknowledge what they have gained from the group To have members identify other supports outside the group that will help them maintain their positive changes	Ask members to share positive changes Ask members to acknowledge value of group Ask members to brainstorm other individuals who will help them maintain positive changes in future Ask group to consider ongoing contact with one another Share in all of the same disclosures asked of membership

TABLE 2.3
Suggestions for Attaining Targeted Group Goals of a Faculty Mentoring Group

Phase of Group	Targeted Group Goal	Suggestions for Attainment
Initial	To have members determine which aspects of their positions are most challenging To have members prioritize which concerns in regard to their positions they want to address To determine common areas of concern about one's position that members want to address	Plan tasks to assist faculty in determining areas of most concern in regard to position Provide task so members are asked to prioritize their areas of concern anonymously Summarize priority list of members' concerns Ask members to vote on common concerns they want to address in group
Middle	To have members delineate in more detail their common areas of concern	Provide systematic way for members to identify important details in regard to areas of concern
	To have members help one another problem solve their concerns	Provide problem-solving method to assist in this process Have members identify what they have control over and what they do in regard to area of concern
	To identify instructions/resources in regard to common concerns	Consider having speakers talk to group Provide relevant resources to address members' concerns Provide members resource list for campus and community
Termination	To have members delineate their positive changes from group To have members identify ways they will be able to maintain positive changes To have members acknowledge how the group has benefitted the entire membership	Have members identify positive changes in one another Identify positive changes in members Ask members to complete a plan to maintain their positive changes and keep it handy for review Have group brainstorm and review ways they can all continue to maintain their positive changes Have members identify the positive changes they have seen in themselves that are most meaningful

Facilitators should remember that at all times during a group they are working simultaneously on two sets of goals: process goals and targeted group goals. For this reason, it is invaluable for a facilitator to understand which set of goals is primary and which set is secondary during each phase of a faculty mentoring group. In addition, as seen in Table 2.1 in the "Primary Focus of Sessions" row, a brief statement for each phase summarizes the primary focus of each phase when taking into consideration the two sets of goals and the primary/secondary emphasis guide.

Facilitators Can Begin and End Groups, but They Cannot Move Groups to the Middle Phase

This is a very important point from the Dennison Group Practice model because it reinforces the idea that groups either bond to a degree that they are ready to begin helping one another work on the concerns or challenges, or they fail to bond to this degree. Facilitators need to keep in mind that some groups, due to any number of factors, are never able to move to the middle phase, or what we might term the *working phase* of the faculty mentoring group. Sometimes members' attendance is so inconsistent that they never feel trusting or bonded enough to move to this phase. In other cases, the composition of personalities in a group is such that the members are not able to trust and open up to one another. Therefore, no matter how skillful the facilitator, some groups will never be able to reach the middle phase regardless of how long they meet. For this reason, facilitators of faculty mentoring groups need to consider ending a faculty mentoring group if they find that a particular group is just not capable of moving to this middle phase. Related to this issue, facilitators will see in the bottom row in Table 2.1 a timing guide that shows the typical length of time a mentoring group spends in each phase. As can be seen, most of these groups are in the initial phase during the fall semester, and then move to the middle phase in spring, and then to the termination phase during the last session.

Joining Members and Increasing Their Bonding Is Intrinsically Valuable

Facilitators must remember that, during the first semester of a new faculty mentoring group, they should always include a relationship-building task at the onset of each session. By carefully planning these relationship-building tasks, facilitators will be able to increase new faculty members' comfort and trust levels in the group. In addition, intentionally planned relationship building ensures that members of the same group open up about themselves at fairly similar levels, which is essential for everyone to feel equally part of a group. To assist with these relationship-building tasks, there is a variety of such tasks in Appendix B.

Facilitators should feel free to use or modify these relationship-building tasks so they are relevant and helpful for a particular group. Always remember, many new faculty members will find that one of the most important benefits of being part of a new faculty

mentoring program is finding a supportive community for oneself and no longer feeling so alone at a new campus. Members repeatedly found such groups to be invaluable in helping them feel there is not something wrong with them or realize they are not the only ones struggling with a particular university policy.

Faculty Mentoring Groups Require a Longer Period for Building Trust Among Their Members Than Does an Individual Mentoring Relationship

Yes, it is true that most faculty members will often open up more quickly with their individual mentors. This is to be expected because the faculty member only has to work on building trust with one person. In contrast, members of the same faculty mentoring group have to develop comfort and trust with all of the members before the same level of group bonding is established. However, group studies have found that once a level of group cohesiveness occurs, then the number of positive changes among the membership far outweighs what most individuals gain from a one-on-one relationship.

Balanced Participation Must Be Established Early on in a Group and Be Maintained Throughout the Group's Existence

It is very important that facilitators require members to participate equally in sessions; otherwise, groups can be places where just a few people do all the talking while others listen. In groups where balanced participation is not established and maintained, facilitators often find attendance problems are frequent and overall interest in the session is low among most members. One of the easy ways to establish balanced participation is to plan a relationship-building task at the onset of each session in which all members are expected to participate. In addition, facilitators may have to move the sharing in a discussion gently but confidently to other participants who have not spoken. Moreover, sometimes it may be necessary to talk outside the group with a faculty member who consistently talks too much or too little during the sessions. Often it is advisable to handle such interactions outside the group so the individual does not feel embarrassed or feels more comfortable to ask questions to clarify the issue of concern.

Sessions Must Be Planned Carefully, Include a Variety of Interventions, and Follow a Format

Junior faculty members are typically very busy professionals who cannot afford to spend time each month in a group unless they feel they are accomplishing something. Therefore, it is essential that facilitators understand the importance of planning all of their group sessions. It is particularly important to plan the initial phase sessions carefully because, during this time in a group, typically fewer members will share and participate. In addition, carefully planning each session helps facilitators go into the group feeling more confident and free to pay more attention to the process of the group (e.g., members' engagement level, any off-task behavior) rather than worrying about what the group is going to discuss. It is a good idea to use a planning sheet (see Appendix E, "Planning Template for Mentoring Group Session," p. 83). In addition, facilitators may want to have a backup plan for the very first meetings of a group since they will not know yet how their group will respond to their initial plan.

Good planning for groups also means trying to provide a variety of interventions, which will serve two purposes. First, in the beginning sessions a variety of interventions often keeps members' interest. Second, by using a variety of interventions, facilitators will be more likely to engage most of the group in discussions and increase the probability that members will find some technique that increases their motivation to try new ways of handling various aspects of their jobs.

In addition to careful planning and variety, facilitators should consider following a format in their sessions. Research on effective groups at any age often has found that group members find that following set formats makes for more comfortable, less anxiety-provoking places for them to share, and often add to the productivity of a group session. A suggested format for mentoring groups might be a three-component routine that begins with a relationship-building task, moves to the main task of addressing some aspect of members' areas of concern or challenge, and ends with each member noting

something positive or helpful about the session. As seen in Appendix E's "Planning Template for Mentoring Group Session" (p. 83), space has been allotted for each of these three parts of a group format.

A wide variety of tasks to use for the various parts of a mentoring group format are provided in the appendices at the end of this book. For example, Appendix B contains tasks for the initial relationship building in each group session. Appendix C contains tasks to elicit members' perspectives about what aspects of their job are most concerning or challenging, which they might want to discuss further in the group, and strategies for addressing participants' common concerns. Appendix D contains closure tasks to end sessions and some that can be used for the termination session. The planning ideas for many of these task sheets can be modified easily and used in one-on-one mentoring sessions.

"In Vivo" Learning Is a Unique Benefit for Faculty Who Participate in a Mentoring Group

In contrast to those in one-on-one mentoring, faculty members who participate in a mentoring group have the opportunity to try out new attitudes and behaviors in front of a peer group. This arena, particularly when it is safe and supportive, can be a more comfortable place for junior faculty members to begin making some important changes in how they handle their position within the college setting. When most individuals have an opportunity to try out new behaviors in front of peers, they are more likely to try those same behaviors outside the group and thus generalize changes they have discussed in group sessions to other settings. Facilitators should think very carefully about how they can create opportunities for members to try out such new behaviors.

The Facilitator's Most Potent Intervention, Particularly in the Initial Phase of a Group, Is the Use of Oneself for Modeling Openness, Warmth, Nonjudgmental Attitude, and Genuine Concern

When beginning faculty mentoring groups, facilitators need to keep in mind that many times the members will either not know one another or have had limited opportunity to get to know one another. For this reason, facilitators need to keep in mind how important their role is in a beginning group. Facilitators clearly set the stage for how supportive, open, genuine, and accepting a group will be to its members. Truly one of the most potent interventions for facilitators to use in a beginning group is themselves. They need to be willing to participate in the relationship-building tasks and even consider being the first to share so they let members know that they are willing to open up in the same way they are asking members to open up. Sometimes members will actually stay in a group during the initial sessions primarily because of the facilitator's warmth, openness, acceptance, and support.

Guidelines for Setting Up Effective Mentoring Groups

Typically there are more issues to address when setting up effective mentoring groups than there are when setting up individual mentoring relationships. Following are guidelines facilitators should keep in mind when setting up these groups.

- It is ideal to meet with each potential member of the group ahead of time to ensure that he or she is motivated and is committed to attending all of the mentoring group sessions.
- Sometimes it is a good idea to have all potential members of these groups sign a contract (sample in Appendix E, p. 84) before the first session that outlines their commitment to attendance, reviews the rules of the group (e.g., attend all sessions, be on time and stay until the end of each session, participate fully in sessions, and keep all information shared during the sessions confidential), and begins to identify what issues they would like to discuss in the group.
- An ideal size for most groups is eight people, and, if at all possible, facilitators should try to have a mixture of men and women, faculty from various schools on campus, and faculty of various ethnicities in any one group. It is not a good idea to have all group members

be of a single gender or ethnicity. However, sometimes this cannot be avoided depending on the composition of faculty members involved in a new faculty mentoring program in any given year.

- Determine a consistent meeting place that will be convenient for all members, is comfortable, and will allow for privacy of these group sessions.
- Ideally two facilitators will meet with each group since this team approach helps address a number of issues. It allows one facilitator to take the lead in a session while the other concentrates on monitoring the process of the group. Two facilitators can provide extra places where difficult or needy faculty members can sit next to these individuals. Also, this team approach can provide increased opportunities for facilitators to model and share for the rest of the group members, and two facilitators can share in planning sessions and preparing materials.
- From the mentoring group at our university, we have found it helpful to plan all the meeting dates of group meetings for the first semester. Typically faculty members' teaching schedules change each semester, so it is best to try to plan the fall semester in the summer and plan the spring in late fall.
- Cofacilitators need to be sure to include time to process after each group session, plan the next session, and prepare related materials. It is very important that facilitating teams do these three tasks consistently so the two facilitators can coordinate their running of these groups.
- At least one of the facilitators should have some extra time available at the end of each group session in case he or she needs to meet with a faculty member to address issues/questions in more depth or to address concerns about that individual's behavior in the group.
- Determine the best meeting time and length with all group members. This can be a very challenging task, and facilitators should expect that some members will have to miss group

sessions because of unexpected issues that arise. We have found that most new faculty members can make a commitment to meeting with their mentoring group once a month for about an hour and a half to two hours.

- Try to run only time-limited, closed groups, which means the membership changes perhaps only at the end of a semester. By ensuring that a group has four to five sessions with the same members, facilitators are able to help groups continue to develop their cohesiveness. For members to feel comfortable sharing their problems and helping one another resolve problems, it is essential to maintain stability in the membership. If group membership changes too frequently, facilitators will often find they have attendance problems and members begin to lose interest in the group.

Guidelines for Planning Effective Mentoring Groups

- Effective group sessions do not often just happen spontaneously; they must be carefully planned, particularly in the beginning sessions of a new mentoring group.
- Cofacilitators should plan each part of their group format very carefully and in great detail, particularly with beginning groups. Consider using the "Planning Template for Mentoring Group Sessions" found in Appendix E (p. 83) to ensure that facilitators plan each component of a group session.
- Sometimes it is helpful to find out members' free-time interests in pre-group sessions. This disclosure can provide some guidance for the type of tasks that might be of interest to junior faculty members.
- All materials related to the group plan should be prepared ahead of time.
- It is a good idea to have a backup plan for the initial sessions of a mentoring group just in case a plan does not appear to be effective with a particular group.

- Facilitators should feel free to consider their own interests and style as they plan their group sessions. Facilitators' enthusiasm for a particular plan will be contagious and actually increase members' engagement in the plan.
- It is a good idea to plan a variety of tasks, particularly during the initial sessions of a group. By following a format, a facilitator can feel comfortable in planning a variety of tasks for each part of a session.
- It is usually not a good idea to plan more than a few sessions in advance since facilitators always want to consider what is going on in a group before planning future sessions.
- Cofacilitators should process a group session immediately after it ends to remember any key points that surfaced, and cofacilitators should consider this processing as they develop their next session plan.

Guidelines for Effectively Facilitating Mentoring Groups

The facilitating of a group will vary depending on the group composition, the styles of the cofacilitators, and the phase of the group. For this reason, cofacilitators should process not just a group's reaction to a session plan but also members' reaction to their facilitation style. Here are additional important guidelines to keep in mind when facilitating mentoring groups.

- Facilitators typically have to be more directive in the beginning group sessions to ensure that all members follow rules and stay on task.
- If facilitators find they have particularly demanding or needy junior faculty members in a group, it can be helpful to make it a point to sit next to such individuals. Sometimes this seating arrangement can help such group members feel less needy or demanding and can offer facilitators a nonverbal way of keeping them on task (e.g., patting the person on the back, or nonverbally asking him or her to not cut off someone else in the group).

- Facilitators often know a group is moving to the middle phase when they find they have to intervene less often to keep a group on task or direct the members through each part of a format.
- Facilitators should use themselves as models in mentoring groups by sharing during the relationship-building tasks in the initial phase and pointing out members' progress during the termination session.
- Facilitators should always keep in mind that they can teach much to their group members just by modeling and sharing some of their own struggles as junior faculty members.

Facilitators should try to point out commonalities among the membership, particularly in the initial phase of a group. Surfacing commonalities is one way a group's members bond.

References

Cox, M. (1999). Peer consultation and faculty learning communities. *New Directions for Teaching and Learning, 1999*(79), 39–49.

Dennison, S. (1989). *Twelve counseling programs for children at risk.* Springfield, IL: Charles C. Thomas.

Yalom, E. (1985). *The theory and practice of group psychotherapy.* New York: Basic Books.

CHAPTER 3

New Faculty Tips on Having a Successful Mentoring Experience

"I valued having access to someone who knows the ropes around campus, especially for managing things like service requirements, and general work-life balance. In my case, the mentor functioned like a wise person to whom I could go for friendly advice."

—Mentee comment

If you are reading this chapter, then you have already decided to pursue mentoring or are considering whether mentoring is worth the time and effort. Perhaps you are concerned that if you ask for mentoring, you will be seen as needy or incompetent. In our experience, the new faculty members who pursue mentoring are very successful people who never miss an opportunity to improve their careers. If you search online for "tips for new faculty," every article or list will include mentoring. You will find that a good mentoring relationship can support you in clarifying your needs and help you strategize ways to meet your goals. This chapter will help you develop realistic expectations for the mentoring relationship, and it offers other ideas for benefits you may not have expected.

Regardless of how successful you have been through your doctoral program, postdoctorate, or other interim employment, you will find that university life is very different. The academic life often puts us alone in our classrooms, our offices, and labs, so many new faculty members feel a sense of isolation on campus. New faculty typically feel swamped with teaching responsibilities and find themselves facing the constant new deadlines of classes and exams, leaving little time for writing up their research. The other stressor many new faculty members experience is the imposter syndrome,

the sneaking dread that you aren't really ready for this and that someone will find out. This feeling is common to most people starting something new and momentous. Don't worry; it will go away.

It might be helpful here to list the characteristics of quick starters:

- They get connected across campus.
- Their work habits reflect goals.
- They write three or more times per week.
- They strategically plan service commitments.
- They seek multiple mentors.

As a new faculty member, you will have some typical needs during your first year or two that reflect the issues we raised here. You need to make connections, both within and outside your department. Although you can think of several work-related reasons for this, a sense of collegiality and community is essential to a successful and happy career. You will have so many new responsibilities that it will be helpful to have someone who has been where you are to help you prioritize them and develop the time management skills to keep you productive rather than panicked. A mentor can help you determine the right balance of time spent on teaching and research for your department and institution. Last, but by no means least, a mentor can give you permission to take care of yourself and maintain the work/life balance that prevents burnout.

When you choose to pursue mentoring, you are making a solid commitment to spend the time necessary on the mentoring relationship to receive the full benefit and to repay your mentor for his or her commitment to support you. If you are in a group mentoring situation, then it is important to realize that your commitment to that group is crucial to the success of the group. Part of that commitment is to the confidentiality (see "New Faculty Mentoring Program Statement of Commitment and Confidentiality," Appendix F, p. 97) of conversations that occur with your mentor or in the group. You will appreciate that the space you create together is safe for disclosure.

Selection of a Mentor

The most important factor in a successful mentoring relationship is a good fit with your mentor. You will need to have a trusting relationship. As your needs change over time, you will change mentors, so you will have multiple mentors. You may also have one mentor for teaching and another for research. This multiple-mentor process is designed to give you what you need when you need it. Ideally, you will have input into who your mentor is, although your department head may assign a mentor for your first year. This first mentor will help you to understand the department, from

processes to culture, and to establish some initial planning and time management tasks (see Sidebar 3.1).

You do need to consider your personality and communication style. We find that both mentors and mentees come in two varieties: either they want their meetings to be all business and strictly focused on the path to tenure, or they appreciate spending some of the time on relaxed conversation and life balance issues. Do you want someone who is the same as or the opposite of who you are? If you tend to let things slide, you may want someone who will hold your feet to the fire. If you work until you drop, you might benefit from someone who will tell you to take care of yourself.

There are benefits to having different mentors as you progress toward tenure. A five- to six-year relationship can get stale, and it is a large commitment to ask of someone. If your department is large enough, having one mentor for your first year, then another to take you up to reappointment, and a third to take you the rest of the way to tenure allows you to discuss your research with at least three senior faculty members in your department. It will be helpful to have people on your tenure committee who have had the time to talk with you and understand your research. If it is a large department, you might want to have a different person each year, though that may make a good fit with each person less likely. You will find it helpful to get different points of view on your work, and it is good to know what expectations each senior faculty member has for your tenure dossier.

You will also benefit from having a mentor outside your department. If your university has a campus-wide mentoring program, you can find an outside mentor through that program. If not, ask your department head to help you find someone. It is important that you have someone outside the department to talk with about things you may not feel comfortable discussing with a colleague inside your department. There is no way around the fact that the mentor in your department will be voting on your tenure some day, and you may not wish to share all of your concerns with that person.

In each case, it would be helpful to have the opportunity to talk briefly with a potential mentor to get a sense of whether this would be a good fit for you. It doesn't have to be a long conversation; for our university-wide mentoring program, we use a

---

SIDEBAR 3.1

Questions to ask yourself as you seek a mentor

- Why have I chosen to do my work in the academy?
- What will be my contribution in my field?
- What is my trajectory?
- How is my fit in my department?
- How do I find community in my work?
- What is my projected image?

five-minute speed meet event. So, prepare an elevator talk about yourself that includes questions about potential mentors and use it when you meet colleagues in or outside your department. Then file away potentially good matches for future consideration. Another possibility is to ask a potential next mentor for advice on a particular matter and see how it goes.

What to Expect

Initially you will want to get to know your mentor. What are his or her areas of expertise in teaching? In research? What are your mentor's outside interests? If you are young and juggling the responsibilities of work and a family, has your mentor been through that experience? At your first meeting with your mentor, you will also want to establish expectations on both sides. It is important to establish the boundaries of the relationship within which you will both feel comfortable meeting your needs (see Sidebar 3.2).

Here are some questions you will want to ask:

- How often will you meet?
- How long will the meetings be?
- Will you have e-mail contact between meetings?
- Can you ask advice for a spur-of-the-moment concern?
- Can you attend university events together?

The second order of business will be a needs assessment. There is a needs assessment checklist in

Appendix C (p. 72). You can fill it out before your first meeting, or make it an assignment for the second meeting. It is a good idea to do this with each new mentor because your needs will change, and each mentor may be able to help you address different needs. You will be the driving force behind what you and your mentor choose to talk about, but ask your mentor to question you as well; he or she may be aware of issues that are not on your radar. One good use you can make of each mentor is to have him or her hold you accountable to accomplish something between meetings and ask you about it. This will be particularly useful regarding your writing, since teaching and departmental responsibilities have regular deadlines, and it is easy to put off writing time. Writing is part of your job description and should be scheduled just like class time. If you use a digital calendar that others can see, they will know that you are busy at that time and be less likely to ask you to attend a meeting.

We recommend coffee meetings for 90 minutes. Lunch and dinner meetings require too much time spent eating and ordering food. If this is your first year as a professor, and you have a mentor in your department, you might want to meet every couple of weeks for the first month or so. After that, monthly meetings should be adequate for the first year. You might also attend university events together; this will be helpful as you will not feel so isolated and your mentor can introduce you to people. Another good activity is to observe your mentor teaching, and have your mentor provide a formative assessment of your teaching (rather than a summative assessment, which involves judging the quality of your teaching for your department head). If such summative assessments are part of your departmental mentor's duties, then ask for several formative assessments, so your mentor can write a summative assessment that includes growth during the year.

You will probably find that, as the year goes on, you need to meet with your mentor less. This is a natural progression in our experience and serves as an indicator that soon you will move on to a new mentor. Ask your current mentor for advice on this; discuss the possibilities in terms of your current and expected needs. As your formal relationship ends, ask whether

---

SIDEBAR 3.2

Get the most out of a mentoring relationship

- Meet regularly.
- Set boundaries.
- Set goals.
- Prepare for meetings.
- E-mail a summary of each meeting.
- Keep a mentoring journal.

you can contact him or her in the future, or whether you might meet for coffee once a year. Regular meetings can keep a former mentor who will vote on your tenure up to date with developments in your work.

Participation in a Mentoring Group

Faculty members at our university greatly appreciate participating in a mentoring group with other new faculty members across campus. As these groups are meant to be support groups, the size of the group should not be more than six to eight. With a small number of people, each member of the group can have the opportunity to speak. If you are going to participate in such a group, it is crucial that you make a commitment to be at every session. A group in which the participants change every week will not bond well and will be a disappointing experience. The other commitment you all must make is to confidentiality (see Appendix F, p. 97), so that everyone will be comfortable sharing concerns openly.

Mentees report that participating in these cross-disciplinary groups gave them a broader perspective of the university community. They also found that it was very illuminating to hear that others were having the same concerns and that they weren't alone in their worries or stressors. Participants were also very happy to get to know other new faculty across campus, which gave them friends with whom to attend events or have coffee, and got them out of their offices and the small world of their departments. They valued sharing ideas, strategies, and experiences. If the group is composed of some first-, second-, and even third-year new faculty, the more experienced members can share tips with the newer faculty. Friendships made in these groups continue past the formal program.

If your university does not provide group mentoring, you may wish to create your own group. Here we describe how the groups work to let you know what to expect, or to help with your efforts if you are developing your own group. The first session of these groups is usually devoted in part to some getting-to-know-you activities. There are many ideas for these icebreakers, which can be found in Appendix B. You may want to use one at the beginning of each meeting. Since

mutual support is part of the function of these groups, the beginning of each session will be devoted to a go-around so that all members can talk briefly about how their month has gone or about an anticipated event.

Although ideally there are senior faculty group facilitators, the group members will determine the focus of each session. The group may complete Appendix C's "Needs Assessment for New Faculty" checklist (p. 72) to help determine discussion topics on which they can agree. Sometimes you will have a common concern and plan ahead to bring in someone to facilitate the discussion around that topic. You may find that some people prefer to have a structured format every time, while others prefer an open discussion about whatever comes up that month. These types of things should be discussed at the first meeting so you can meet everyone's needs at least some of the time.

We highly recommend that you participate in a mentoring group. Here is how one participant responded to a question about unforeseen benefits:

- Learning from everyone else's experiences—I learned so many useful tips and strategies from the other new faculty and the facilitators that I wouldn't have even known to ask about.
- Participating in the Learning Community also helped me to normalize my experiences—for example, almost everyone in the group mentioned feeling like they were slow writers, and almost everyone had a similar experience of feeling heavily recruited when we were interviewing but then no one stopping by to welcome us once they actually arrived [i.e., it's nothing personal; everyone is just really busy, so you have to make an effort to get to know people in your department].

Self-Assessment of Your Mentoring Experience

You need to take the time to assess how your mentoring experience went at the end of each formalized relationship for two reasons. The person who set up the program, whether it is university-wide or departmental, will need to know what worked and what did not.

Providing feedback to him or her helps to improve the program in the future. If it is within your department, then it will also improve your continuing program. You will find a suggested form to help you do this in Appendix G (p. 100).

You probably will want to do some kind of informal assessment at least midway through your year in a mentoring relationship. What is going well, that you want to continue? What is proving to be less than helpful, that you'd like to stop? What is missing that you need to start addressing? Take a look at the goals you set for yourself. Is the experience meeting your expectations? Were your expectations realistic?

Taking careful stock of the experience at the end of each year will help you choose your next mentor and plan what you want to get out of your next mentoring experience. If you are lucky enough to be participating in both one-on-one mentoring and group mentoring, ask yourself which of your main goals are being met by each type of mentoring, and how much of your attainment of those goals is due to your own efforts. You can think of this as three legs of a tripod of support for a fulfilling, successful career.

Show gratitude to your mentor. If your mentor gives you some advice that turns out to be just what you needed, then tell him or her so and say thank you. You will probably find that there are ways you can help your mentor as well, so that the relationship is reciprocal. This is the ideal mentoring relationship.

CHAPTER 4

Tips for Guidance of Departmental Mentoring

"I valued most the advice my mentor gave on research and how to move past obstacles to improve productivity. I also valued my mentor's advice on how to balance the numerous responsibilities of being an assistant professor and how to balance life outside work with life at work."

—Mentee comment

The material contained in this chapter is intended for department chairs/heads and is relevant primarily to one-on-one mentoring relationships. However, the guidelines in this part of the manual can be modified easily for two types of mentoring relationships—(a) mentors from within a mentee's department and (b) mentors from another department within the same school/unit or even from another unit on the same campus. In fact, some universities report assigning mentors from outside a mentee's university for various reasons, but most frequently because of a lack of a good match within the department in terms of gender, research area, and/or ethnicity. You will find that much of the material in this chapter can be modified easily to meet the specific needs of any of these one-on-one mentoring relationships.

Importance of Formal Mentoring of New Faculty

Essentially mentoring is viewed as senior faculty members assisting junior faculty members in their development on both professional and personal levels. As indicated in the literature review in chapter 7, many departments seek to increase the diversity of their faculty in gender, ethnicity/national origin, and/or area of research and teaching expertise. More formal mentoring programs address the need to recruit and retain minority faculty.

When we interviewed a number of our university department chairs/heads who have had long-standing formal mentoring programs within their departments, several major themes emerged. These higher education middle managers noted how important formal mentoring is to creating a community within their departments that is welcoming, respectful, and inclusive of all faculty members. These chairs also spoke about the value of creating a mentoring culture within their departments in which everyone is viewed as being both a learner and teacher/supporter of others. By valuing the informal and formal mentoring of all faculty members, the department is seen as placing a high value on this role and then carrying it out intentionally to mentor junior faculty. It is interesting that these chairs also noted that the formal mentoring program within their respective departments has helped ensure that new faculty members are involved in most major decision making, which has facilitated the efficiency of the process.

Another way in which mentoring contributes to departmental culture is the practice of one senior faculty member being responsible to protect and advocate for a new faculty member. Some of the department chairs noted that, over time, they have seen how much it means to their junior faculty members to know they have at least one senior faculty member on their side as they continue to orient themselves to the university and become more familiar with the expectations of their faculty position. In addition, some of the chairs reported that, because of their mentoring program, they believe there is more collaboration between junior and senior faculty in securing external funds, carrying out research, and publishing articles. Two chairs in particular also pointed out that formal mentoring ensured that new faculty members' progress toward tenure and promotion is always monitored. Readers are referred to Sidebar 4.1, which lists what Sorcinelli (2000) delineated as the 10 principles for

good practice within a higher education department. It is not surprising that these 10 principles further validate the tremendous multiple benefits of creating a formal mentoring program within a department.

Logistics for Establishing a Departmental Mentoring Program

Several components need to be planned and carried out for a department to have a successful mentoring program. First and foremost, chairs/heads should determine whether there is a policy statement at the university level and/or school level that allows for establishing a mentoring program. If such a policy does not exist, it is a good idea to create one, and then go through the usual steps to have it approved at either the university or school level. With a policy statement in place, chairs can be more assured that they have the endorsement of and resource support from the university's upper administration and/or their dean. In addition, some chairs may feel it would be important as well to have a departmental policy statement on their mentoring program so that the mentoring opportunity/support provided to all new faculty members is more consistent across the board. Such a policy should also include details about the mentoring support so new chairs will be able to continue the mentoring practice already in place.

A second logistical issue that has to be addressed is matching new faculty with senior faculty who will serve as mentors. Most researchers in this area advise that it is best that both the mentee and mentor have input into this matching. In addition, new faculty members should know that mentoring is optional so they feel they have a choice about participating in such a program. Departmental chairs/heads will have to decide how they will make match decisions. Sidebar 4.2 provides some helpful ideas on the qualities of effective mentors. Even though a number of authors in the related literature advise formally training mentors, often a departmental chair will not have the time, money, or expertise to provide such formal training. As a result, chairs may have to ask senior faculty members who already have some of the qualities listed in Sidebar

---

SIDEBAR 4.1

Sorcinelli's (2000) 10 principles for good practice

1. Good practice communicates expectations for performance.

2. Good practice gives feedback on performance.

3. Good practice enhances collegial review processes.

4. Good practice creates flexible timelines for tenure.

5. Good practice encourages mentoring by senior faculty.

6. Good practice extends mentoring and feedback to graduate students who aspire to be faculty members.

7. Good practice recognizes the department chair as a career sponsor.

8. Good practice supports teaching, particularly at the undergraduate level.

9. Good practice supports scholarly development.

10. Good practice fosters a balance between professional and personal life.

SIDEBAR 4.2

Characteristics of effective mentors

- Good listener
- Organizational skills
- Willingness to promote others
- Ability to support
- Ability to challenge
- Reliability
- Collaborative skills
- Insightful

4.2. If there is a university or unit policy on mentoring, training may be available as a resource. A mentor training session is outlined in Appendix I (p. 120).

As mentioned earlier, it is also a good idea to ask the new faculty member if he or she would prefer a particular senior faculty member as mentor. Department heads must also be sensitive to the challenges involved when they make cross-gender matches or matches where the mentor is not of the same ethnicity as the mentee. This point is delineated further in the section in this chapter under challenges of departmental mentoring. In brief, it is ideal, although most times not practical, to make mentoring matches where the pairs are of the same gender and ethnicity. It should be noted here, however, that most of our mentees over a five-year period did report they received effective mentoring from senior faculty who were not the same gender and/or ethnicity. It appears from the related literature that the area of mentoring that is not perceived as effective in such cases involves more of the psychosocial or personal needs of the mentee. In such cases, chairs may decide to match a new faculty member with someone from another department either within the same school or another unit on campus. Even though such a senior faculty member will have the disadvantage of not being as knowledgeable about tenure requirements and other procedures within the mentee's department, the benefits of matching a junior faculty member with someone

of the same gender and ethnicity may outweigh the disadvantages.

A third logical issue involves the time commitment for a mentoring match within a department. Department chairs will have to determine, possibly with input from both senior and junior faculty members, how long mentoring matches should last. Much of the recent literature favors new faculty having multiple mentors while they work toward tenure and promotion. In addition, some studies have found that mentors prefer a shorter time commitment since they report having more energy and enthusiasm for a one-year commitment than a five-year one. It will be critical that chairs define the time commitment for making these matches so the mentor and mentee are clear on this point. If chairs decide to follow a one-year format for mentoring matches, then they will have to follow a similar process when making mentoring matches the following years until a junior faculty member is tenured and promoted. One of the many advantages of a junior faculty member being matched with several senior faculty members is that this gives the junior faculty member an opportunity to learn from the strengths of each person and even to consider some collaborative work with one or more of them. A second advantage is the input received will come from many of the people who will be participating in tenure decisions.

The fourth logistical issue that will need to be addressed is the chair's monitoring of the mentoring process. Even if the match is made for one year, the chair still needs to plan some intentional way of checking on the level of effectiveness of the mentoring before the end of the year. Department heads should check with the mentee and mentor at least at the end of each semester. Chairs can do this monitoring informally by simply asking each person involved in the match how well he or she feels the mentoring is meeting the mentee's needs and goals. Another option is a "Departmental Mentoring Checklist" (Appendix H, p. 108), which allows the mentoring pair to decide on goals for the year and evaluate progress. In addition to checking on the effectiveness of this mentoring, chairs need to ensure that there is regular contact between the mentor and mentee. During the first semester of mentoring a new faculty member, the mentor will need to meet once a week with the mentee, at least for the first month or two. However, during the second and following semesters, there can be fewer of these meetings since the mentee may not need to consult with the mentor as often. Sometimes the chair may have to give the mentor suggestions for other ways to support the mentee, such as peer evaluations of his or her teaching, review of manuscripts, suggestions for others who could review grant proposals or manuscripts, and recommendations for journals to consider for submission of articles.

The fifth logistical issue that needs to be planned for a departmental mentoring program is evaluating its efficacy. Chairs will need to keep in mind that in many small departments it will be difficult if not impossible for new faculty members to feel comfortable enough to share their evaluation of their assigned mentors honestly. This is particularly true since senior faculty mentors from one's own department will ultimately vote on the mentee's tenure. Then, we suggest that department chairs work in collaboration with chairs from other departments and their dean so that evaluating the mentoring of new faculty can be done anonymously across the entire school or unit. A standard survey can be developed and then distributed to all new faculty who have mentors. When these surveys have been completed and collected, aggregated data can be analyzed, with the results reported for the entire school or unit rather than for a particular department. The larger unit can then take necessary measures, such as providing mentor training, to improve mentoring. Chairs need to be sensitive to the fact that mentees need to have a safe way to provide formal feedback on the effectiveness of their mentoring support at least once a year. If a school decides to use this type of evaluation method, then individual chairs should still meet separately with both the mentors and mentees to ask more informally how they evaluate the mentoring experience. Chairs will need to use data gathered from all evaluation methods to inform how they proceed with each new faculty member's mentoring in the future.

Benefits of Departmental Mentoring for Junior and Senior Faculty Members

In the chapter 7 review of the literature, many benefits are reported from providing a formalized mentoring program to new faculty members. Benefits that primarily address current needs of most higher education institutions include, but are not limited to: recruitment of high-quality, diverse faculty members; retention of these faculty members; cost savings from not having to orient and train new faculty; and preservation of a department's mission, culture, and norms. In addition, formal mentoring can provide the following valuable benefits for a department:

- Assists minority faculty in addressing issues unique to their faculty role
- Enhances junior faculty members' teaching skills by providing peer reviews of their teaching, or allowing the mentees to observe the mentors' teaching
- Improves new faculty members' ability to secure external funding
- Increases new faculty members' skills in research, writing, and publication of manuscripts
- Increases the overall productivity of new faculty members
- Improves new faculty members' skills in preparing online courses and teaching them
- Increases junior faculty members' career satisfaction and ability to raise their profile
- Provides assistance so new faculty members are able to find a satisfying work/personal life balance
- Assists new faculty members in assimilating into a department and finding a sense of community within this setting, thus ensuring the continuity of a culture within the department
- Provides much-needed guidance in prioritizing and balancing the many demands on a new faculty member
- Creates more of a sense of community within a department
- Provides more built-in protection and advocacy safeguards for new faculty members
- Increases the potential of collaboration between colleagues within a department in securing external funding and publishing manuscripts
- Improves junior faculty members' success in attaining tenure and promotion, often

assisting them with the preparation of their three-year and final-year dossier

- Provides a safe place for new faculty members to air their concerns, questions, and/or challenges
- Regularly informs senior faculty about how they are supporting new faculty and what changes, if any, could be beneficial

Refer to chapter 7 for specific literature citations supporting many of these benefits of formalized departmental mentoring programs. Be aware, however, that some of the benefits listed here surfaced from our interviews with department heads/chairs who have had a long history of formal mentoring within their respective departments.

Challenges of Departmental Mentoring

There is no doubt that in most departments the benefits of providing a formal mentoring program to all new faculty members far outweigh the challenges involved in establishing and conducting this type of support. The following challenges are addressed in the literature (see chapter 7 for related literature) and/or were identified from our interviews with departmental chairs/heads.

- One of the most frequently reported challenges involves whether both the mentor and mentee are willing and able to make the time commitment for regular mentoring sessions. Chairs should check with senior faculty before making a match for a new faculty member, to ensure that a particular senior faculty member is able to make the time commitment needed to mentor someone effectively.
- Related to the first challenge, chairs need to advocate for recognizing the time and effort involved in mentoring. In terms of university service, it is important that this role is able to be documented in a mentor's annual report and also in his or her dossier when the individual is up for promotion. There is a signature sheet in Appendix F (p. 92) that can be used to clear a faculty member to participate in a school or university mentoring program that can also

document the mentoring service. If promotion and tenure documents are being revised, advocate for the inclusion of recognition for mentoring.

- Since there will always be a power differential when a senior faculty member mentors a junior faculty member, it is important to remember that the new faculty member may not always feel comfortable sharing his or her concerns, challenges, or problems honestly. For this reason, some chairs may decide to match new faculty with mentors from other departments within either their school or university, at least for the first year.
- Sometimes only a few senior faculty members are available to serve as mentors for a particular department. In such cases, a chair may decide to consider asking a senior faculty member from another department to serve in this role.
- Although it is ideal to rotate mentoring of new faculty members every year or two until they attain tenure and promotion, there may not be enough senior faculty members in a department to allow for this. In this case, chairs may want to seek a mentor for a new faculty member from another department.
- The mentoring match may not work well for any number of reasons, including lack of time commitment on either party's part, personality conflicts, and/or a match that involves different genders and/or ethnicities. Chairs must be sensitive to the possibility that a new faculty member, of a different gender and/or ethnicity from his or her mentor, may not feel comfortable sharing some things with a particular mentor. Sidebar 4.3 delineates some of the threats to promotion and tenure that Yoshinaga-Itano (2006) identified for minority faculty members who are often represented in small numbers in most departments.
- Not all senior faculty members are naturally good mentors and, in some cases, some of them could benefit from formal training on the mentoring role. One added challenge is that the literature contains very little information on what such a training program should involve. In addition, many chairs may

---

SIDEBAR 4.3

Threats to promotion and tenure of minority faculty members

- More likely to have nontraditional areas of scholarship

- More likely to have nontraditional venues of publication

- More likely to be in applied areas of research that will take longer to complete

- Lack of adequate research mentors

- Lack of senior faculty understanding of scholarship challenges for minority faculty

- Lack of an equitable evaluation system

- Lack of knowledge of the political systems in a university and steps necessary to become tenured

- Lack of mentors for psychosocial supports

- Lack of senior faculty familiar with the challenges minority faculty face in the classroom

- Lack of awareness that minority faculty often have higher levels of service

---

not have the resources to provide such training. One alternative way to provide training of senior faculty for mentoring roles is for a chair to request that his or her dean address this issue from the school budget.

- Continuity and consistency in how a departmental mentoring program is conducted can be a challenge, particularly with changing department chairs. For this reason, we recommend that all senior faculty work together to establish a policy and related procedures for conducting mentoring within their department. If such information is in writing, and all involved senior faculty have agreed to it, there is less likelihood that there will be problems with continuity and consistency with a department's mentoring program even when new chairs are named.

- Another challenge involves getting regular feedback from a mentee about how the mentoring relationship is working. As indicated earlier, it is very important to plan ways to seek such feedback at the end of each semester and then at the end of each year. The checklist in Appendix H (p. 108) can be used both to plan the year's mentoring activities and report on accomplishments during the year. It is also essential that this feedback be elicited in such a way that new faculty members feel they can share honestly how the mentoring support is working from their perspective.

Stages of Professional Development

Obviously every new faculty member needs to be treated as an individual; however, we have found that there appear to be fairly common stages of professional development these professionals typically experience within a department. Following are those stages with some of the more common concerns and goals identified in each stage, along with the ideal way to make the mentoring matches.

Initial Year

Common concerns/goals for a new faculty member include:

- dealing with the imposter syndrome;
- having a fragile sense of competency for job responsibilities;
- wanting to feel a sense of belonging in a department;
- being overwhelmed with various tasks;
- experiencing challenges in balancing time for all role expectations;
- worrying about making mistakes and not doing well;
- publishing the dissertation; and
- setting the research agenda/setting up a lab.

The department chair has many opportunities to support a new faculty member outside of helping in the search for a mentor. The single most important support the chair can give is protecting the new faculty member's time. New faculty should be guided to service assignments that are not time intensive (see "Time Commitment for Faculty Senate Committees," Appendix H, p. 110), and should be advised to respond to requests for their time by saying, "That sounds very interesting. I'll need to check with my chair on that."

The ideal way to match a new faculty member with a mentor is for the two people involved to decide mutually to work together. However, for a first-semester hire, this may not be possible. In this case the chair will make the decision while considering the many factors mentioned in this chapter. Most new faculty will not know senior faculty members well enough at this stage to indicate whom they would like as a mentor.

Years Two to Three

Common issues/goals for new faculty members during these next two years include:

- establishing a clear research program;
- becoming more competent as a classroom instructor;
- determining a balance and schedule for completing all that is necessary for progressing toward tenure;
- wanting to establish more of a work/personal life balance;
- increasing their network of connections within the department and in the wider university;
- often feeling ready for more autonomy due to increased self-confidence; and
- preparing a dossier for successful reappointment at the three-year mark.

During these two years, new faculty members should be asked to indicate whom they would like as their mentor. A chair may not always be able to honor this request, but it is important that these professionals have a say in the match during this stage. Mentoring pairs who participate in the choice will be more committed to spending the time and effort required to have a successful relationship.

Years Four to Six

Common issues/goals for new faculty members in this stage include:

- the need to increase their profile in the department, university, and research area;
- often a major push to secure external funds for research;
- high motivation to increase publications in preparation for tenure review;
- the need to have senior faculty/chair review curriculum vitae to see how they are progressing toward tenure in the department; and
- preparation of the dossier for successful tenure and promotion review.

Ideally by this point in a new faculty member's career, the chair should allow this person to determine again who would be his or her choice for a good mentor, whether someone inside or outside the department. Again, the chair may not be able to honor this request due to the workload of the prospective mentor, but it is most important to respect these professionals' perspectives on what type of mentor they need during these last years before they are up for tenure review.

Assessment of a Departmental Mentoring Program

As indicated earlier, it is most important for a chair to have access to or create both formative and summative methods for evaluating a new faculty mentoring program. Sometimes the formative evaluation can be done more informally, typically at the end of each semester, by the chair asking both the mentee and mentor how they view their working together. It is ideal to explore how this mentoring is working with both the mentee and mentor present so any issues of concern can be addressed immediately. In addition, this type of meeting provides mentees with an opportunity to provide positive feedback to their mentors; the same is true to enable the mentor to provide similar feedback to the mentee. A planning and assessment checklist of areas of focus during the coming year, as well as for indicating that the work was addressed, is in Appendix H (p. 108).

It is also important that both mentor and mentee complete a more formal summative evaluation each year. This type of evaluation should be conducted at the school/unit level rather than the departmental level. The reason is that this method of assessment allows for new faculty members to provide feedback in a more anonymous way that increases their comfort level and makes them more likely to provide honest feedback. Included in Appendix G is a sample summative evaluation form for new faculty members and one for mentors. Chairs should feel free to suggest these sample evaluation surveys or modifications of them to their deans to assist with these assessments at the school/unit level.

Chairs should supplement these evaluations by continuing to seek more informal feedback from both mentees and mentors and from the most recently tenured members of their faculty. These last individuals can share the most helpful support they received as they worked toward tenure and promotion.

References

Sorcinelli, M. (2000). *Principles of good practice: Supporting early-career faculty.* Washington, DC: American Association for Higher Education.

Yoshinaga-Itano, C. (2006). Institutional barriers and myths to recruitment and retention of faculty of color. In C. Stanley (Ed.), *Faculty of color: Teaching in predominantly White colleges and universities.* Boston, MA: Anker.

CHAPTER 5

Guidelines for Administrators

"I want to BE part of the university. This program makes me feel like I'm not just another number."

—Mentee comment

Advantages of a University-Wide Mentoring Program

There are several advantages of running a mentoring program at the university or college level; Figure 5.1 provides an overview of these benefits. First and foremost is the ability to recruit and retain highly qualified and diverse faculty. It is now common for prospective faculty members to ask about mentoring at on-campus interviews, and to indicate that it is a consideration when choosing a position. Formalizing a mentoring program at the university level gives greater access to women and minority faculty members, who tend to be excluded from informal mentoring arrangements (Marvasti, 2005; Skachkova, 2007). The seven-year retention data at our institution for junior faculty participating in a university-wide program versus those who do not indicate that overall retention is 14 percentage points higher for those participating. Among diverse faculty, including minority and international faculty members, the proportion of those who remain is 92%, an astounding 34% higher for participants. Higher retention means lower costs for recruitment and hiring, which, considering advertising, person-hours, and interviews, are at least equal to a year's salary for the new hire (Detmar, 2004). A university-wide program will keep the higher administration abreast of concerns that arise specific to international faculty members, including acculturation and the burden of formal paperwork (e.g., visas, green cards).

The second advantage is in efficiency of management. The numbers of new faculty within smaller units each year is typically not high. Larger numbers of participants lower costs, particularly for recruitment, oversight, management, and assessment of the program. A larger program also provides expanded opportunities to find a successful mentor-mentee match.

Third, these programs provide an orientation to university culture and are an excellent means to transmit the university's mission and identity. Duke University's mentoring policy states that it is essential to the well-being of the institution. A university-wide program is also advantageous because it establishes a formal, consistent structure. Mentoring across departments ranges from nonexistent to formal and intensive. Offering a university-wide program ensures that a minimal level of mentoring is available to all who wish to participate. Such a program by necessity involves mentor pairs who are not in the same department or area of research/teaching; this is very beneficial for the newest faculty members, as it provides a safe person to talk to who will not be voting on their tenure.

This in turn leads to an expanded sense of community on campus. Mentors and mentees in our university-wide program have both reported this to be the case. The broad exposure to colleagues in many disciplines fosters a sense of inclusion and an awareness of other perspectives on campus. It also includes the symbolic benefit that participants feel the university administration cares about them and their success.

Figure 5.1. Benefits of a Campus-Wide Mentoring Program

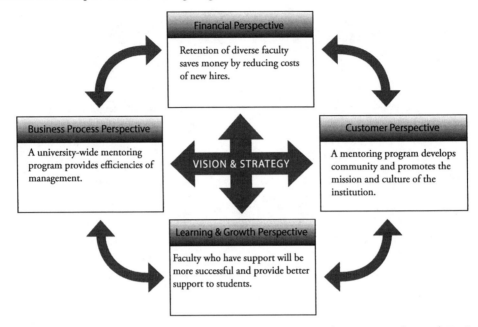

Note. Adapted from *The Balanced Scorecard: Translating Strategy Into Action*, by R. S. Kaplan and D. P. Norton, 1996, figure 1-1. Copyright 1996 by the President and Fellows of Harvard College.

Investments Necessary to Create and Sustain a Program

Visibility is the key component of the successful creation and support of a university-wide program. Such a program must have the visible support of the higher administration; this support comes not only from formal reports and updates to the deans' council, but also from informal conversations wherever possible. The University of Michigan recommends that this take the form of a university-wide statement on mentoring, posted on the provost's website and included in the faculty handbook. Mentoring policies such as those at Duke University are listed in Appendix A. The website should have a link to a faculty mentoring webpage with resources for all involved. Including information about mentoring resources in the letter of offer when hiring a new professor also gives such programs early visibility.

Financial support need not be high, and should not be so high that economic downturns threaten the program's existence. Nevertheless, there are some minimum requirements:

- Support for a director or coordinator in the form of course releases

- Seed money for mentee projects as a small grant ($500 each)
- Marketing support (brochures, website)

The development office can target retired faculty as potential sources of funding for the program.

Providing space, particularly in the form of informal, more intimate meeting space for group meetings, indicates a commitment to the program. It also reinforces a sense of confidentiality and safety for the participants, who have a sense that "this is our space." This, in turn, attaches importance to the program and, therefore, to the participants.

Logistical Support

There are top-down as well as bottom-up considerations. Top-down advancement of the program comes from the provost or president down through the deans, who pass on that visible support to the chairs of their departments. However, the driving force for the program and its development and revision must come from the ranks of professors, associate professors, and assistant professors. Mentor participation should be voluntary. A committee of faculty mentors and mentees could write a university manual for mentoring, to be approved by the Faculty Senate.

"Housing" the program in one unit will provide stability through changes in leadership, both in the program and at higher levels of administration. The unit in which the program is embedded must be identifiable as one that supports faculty development in research and teaching. There should be cross-fertilization of the program with offices dedicated to both teaching and research. Separate programs should be offered to tenure-track, nontenure-track, and adjunct faculty members, as each group has very different needs.

Someone must be at the helm of the program. A person who feels ownership of the program will provide good stewardship. This will be someone with a passion for the work as well as good credentials in teaching and research. Such a person will have credibility with the mentors, mentees, group facilitators, and others on campus who support teaching and research. Group facilitation skills are also very helpful, but an individual can attain these through collaboration with experts in the field on campus (social work, communication studies, counseling).

The development of a cadre of mentors will be one of the first jobs of the program director. Deans can be very helpful in the early solicitation of potential mentors and may wish to have a say in who is considered. On our campus, both the dean and the department head sign off on a memorandum of understanding that recognizes the service commitment involved. Another recruitment source is previous winners of teaching and research awards.

Alternative Program Models: One-on-One, Group, or Both

University-Wide One-on-One Mentoring

In a one-on-one mentoring program, junior faculty members are paired with a senior faculty mentor outside their home department. Some programs recruit new mentors or retain mentors from the previous year during the spring semester. In this case, it is not expected that mentees and mentors will have close research interests, and matches are made based mostly on personality. Typically there is a "meet the mentors" evening, and mentees are permitted to select a few top choices or reject poor matches. The coordinator of the program then creates the matches based on their choices. Other programs recruit new mentees, collect information, and then seek out a mentor with similar interests. Without a faculty database, this would be a daunting task. We recommend that mentors choose to participate, and that mentees have a say in mentor decisions, as a match misfit is the most commonly cited problem (Eby & Lockwood, 2005; Kram & Isabella, 1985). Sidebar 5.1 lists the duties most mentoring program directors are expected to be responsible for. Appendix I contains a more complete job description for a director (p. 118).

Monitoring of these relationships should be done to ensure that the pairs are actually meeting regularly, and that things are going smoothly. The easiest and most efficient way for the coordinator to do this without intruding is to meet monthly with the mentors as a group to talk about how meetings with mentees are going. This has the added benefit of soliciting the collective wisdom in the room about a topic of concern to new faculty. These meetings also provide the coordinator with information that will improve the program. Assessment can occur in two stages. An informal assessment by phone call to the mentee can

---

SIDEBAR 5.1

Coordinator duties

- Recruitment of mentors, group facilitators, and mentees
- Mentor and group facilitator training
- Mentor orientation
- Mentor-mentee pairings
- Facilitating group and mentor monthly meetings
- Managing mini-grant proposals
- Meeting with advisory committee
- Assessment
- Yearly newsletter
- Advise departments on mentoring

occur in the fall to be sure the match is working out well. Then, in the spring, a formal survey assessment can be done with both mentees and mentors.

A university-wide program can also include group mentoring, dividing up the cohort into small groups of six to eight people that are facilitated by two senior faculty members. The following section offers a short description of group programs, and chapter 2 describes the format and facilitation in great detail.

Group Mentoring Programs

Some universities create mentoring groups. The greatest benefits of the group model are the support participants receive and the opportunity to make contacts with colleagues from across campus. These range from fairly informal groups in which junior faculty meet to help each other and share successes, to formal programs where junior faculty are given a course release and a group leader, and are expected to produce a product at the end of the year. An in-between model would be to have junior faculty meet with one or two senior faculty facilitators regularly. How frequently these groups meet can range from weekly to monthly. Weekly meetings can seem like a large time commitment, but if they are used in part as accountability groups for writing, the time commitment is more likely to be well received. Group members can choose to bring in speakers for mini-workshops. We recommend that meetings be 90 minutes in length to give all members a chance to participate in discussions.

Groups that meet with a facilitator can do ongoing assessments or just do one at midterm. A final survey will provide both formative and summative evaluation of the program. Group facilitators should meet regularly with the program coordinator to monitor and improve the program. The coordinator in this instance can inform group facilitators and mentors of developments discerned from each meeting when the program consists of both one-on-one and group mentoring.

Unit-Level Mentoring Programs

Higher levels of administration can support department-level mentoring. Such support can take the form of a consultant to departments on mentoring, who can advise on the development of departmental policy, and also on setting up and managing

departmental mentoring programs. In addition, the consultant can offer workshops and training to mentors and group facilitators. A webpage can provide access to university policy on mentoring and to forms for monitoring and assessment, which will make it easier for department heads to administer and deans to oversee for effectiveness.

A dean's office can also maintain a database of faculty interests and expertise. This information can be used to determine possible matches for mentors outside the new faculty member's department. Multiple mentors over the pre-tenure years are very beneficial, and the database can be used as well to match up senior faculty for peer mentoring post-tenure.

Levels of Support

Each institution will have its own specific needs and resources, so we break down potential levels of support depending on a university/college's resources.

Minimal Support

An administration with no funds available can facilitate support for mentoring by bringing together a committee of faculty to develop a mentoring policy or a faculty development policy that includes mentoring. The committee can develop guidelines for mentors, assessment materials, and training materials, which can be posted on the university or college website. Workshops and training can be embedded in the work of the Teaching and Learning Center and/or the Office of Research. The materials provided, however, must represent the full scope of the new faculty members' responsibilities and address their needs in seeking tenure. Without a point person, this level of support lacks visibility, which will not remedy any uneven quality of mentoring on campus. Without oversight, there will be no ongoing improvements to address changing needs and maintain the seamless continuity of a formal program.

Low Support

A tenured faculty member with one course release can provide a subset of support resources, geared either toward helping departments with internal mentoring or toward some form of university-wide mentoring. In the first case, faculty can provide training programs for mentors and consult with departments on the development of internal policies, as noted previously. Another possibility would be to coordinate a university-wide group mentoring program. This would involve recruiting and training group facilitators, recruiting mentees into the groups, coordinating group schedules and assigning mentees to groups, and meeting regularly with the group facilitators, as well as assessing the program, both formatively and for annual report purposes. A third job description for a one-quarter-time faculty coordinator would be to facilitate a university-wide one-on-one mentoring program, which would include recruiting and training mentors, recruiting mentees, planning a "meet the mentors" event, matching mentoring pairs, meeting monthly with the mentors, and assessing the matches and the overall program.

Moderate Support

A half-time coordinator could provide two of the three possibilities listed above. The coordinator could facilitate both aspects of a university-wide program, providing both one-on-one and group mentoring. Having both aspects is maximally beneficial, as some mentee concerns are not easily discussed in a group. The group provides the level of support that only a peer group can provide, and maximizes connections across campus, a key characteristic of successful new faculty members.

Another possibility would be to provide group mentoring to complement interdepartmental mentoring, or to coordinate intradepartmental mentoring to complement interdepartmental mentoring. The coordinator would also consult with department heads to support their needs.

Full Support

A full-time director of mentoring could accomplish all of the above: consulting with department heads, facilitating university-wide group and individual mentoring, maintaining a database of faculty interests and research, and providing training and workshops throughout the year. This option gives the program the greatest visibility and flexibility and allows focused effort on continuing improvements to the program.

We believe that this level of support would greatly facilitate the development of a culture of mentoring on campus.

Challenges

Although the budget is not large, funding sources must be determined. If the cost is shared among all deans, the office of research, the teaching/learning center, and the provost's or president's office, the burden on each individual unit will be light.

A second challenge is gaining the commitment from participants to the departmental workload, evaluation, and reward system. Administrative expectations must be clear. It is helpful for the units and the university to institute an Excellence in Faculty Mentoring Award to give visibility to a reward system and to faculty mentoring on campus.

There may be weak points in support from school or college-level administrators. A strong proposal outlining the benefits accrued by other mentoring programs may mitigate this reluctance. However, a unit may feel that it provides adequate mentoring in-house. The system for confidentiality must be respected. If mentors find themselves in a position to vote on their mentees' tenure, there should be a system for recusement.

References

Detmar, K. (2004). What we waste when faculty hiring goes wrong. *The Chronicle of Higher Education, 51*(17), 86–88.

Eby, L.T., & Lockwood, A. (2005). Protégés' and mentors' reactions to participating in formal mentoring programs: A qualitative investigation. *Journal of Vocational Behavior, 67*(3), 441–458.

Kram, K. E., & Isabella, L.S. (1985). Mentoring alternatives: The role of peer relationships in career development. *Academy of Management Journal, 28*(1), 110–132.

Marvasti, A. (2005). U.S. academic institutions and perceived effectiveness of foreign-born faculty. *Journal of Economic Issues, 39*(1), 151–176.

Skachkova, P. (2007). Academic careers of immigrant women professors in the U.S. *Higher Education, 53*(6), 697–738.

CHAPTER 6

Advice for the Director of a Faculty Mentoring Program

"In my first years at the university, I was mentored in my department, but this program gave me a better sense of the university and helped me feel a part of the university."

—Mentee comment

If you are reading this chapter, then either you would like to bring a university-wide mentoring program into being, or you have been appointed to do so. This chapter first addresses preparing a proposal for such a program and then describes the director's work in creating and maintaining a program. A more detailed description of proposal development can be found in Phillips, Crane, and Dennison (2010). You will also find a job description for the director in Appendix I (p. 118).

Developing a Proposal for a University-Wide Mentoring Program

Address Stakeholder Concerns

Although the benefits of a university-wide mentoring program are easy to recognize, the case for support for the program must be made with all stakeholders in mind. This will include the provost or president, the deans, the chief financial officer, department heads, and senior faculty. You will need to ascertain the needs and goals of each of these stakeholders, and in your proposal address how the program will meet them. Consider the proposal approval process; who will be contributing to a final decision on the program?

Sources of this information will be mission statements, strategic plans, and accreditation reports. It will be helpful to mention that your accrediting body includes faculty development in its accrediting principles, and that this can be found on its website. Among the potential university goals that a mentoring program can meet include:

- recruitment and retention of good faculty;
- increasing the diversity of faculty;
- increasing the number of international faculty; and
- encouraging interdisciplinary teaching and research.

Assess the Need for Mentoring

There are three critical areas to assess in determining the need for university-wide mentoring. The first is attrition and retention rates for new faculty at your university. Your institutional research office can pull these numbers together for you. We suggest that you request data for about 10 years. These data should include the number of new faculty hired, the number who have left the university before tenure and when (after three years, etc.), and the number who achieved tenure. You will also want to examine these data by gender, race, and foreign national status.

The second critical assessment is the cost of hiring new faculty. A good source of information on the direct costs will be the people who manage budgets in deans' offices. You should obtain this information from at least one such office, although if costs are very different across your university, you might want to establish the range of costs. Direct costs include advertising the position, travel expenses for airport interviews and for campus interviews, recruiting applicants at national conferences, on-campus interview expenses (e.g., meals, hotels), and negotiated start-up costs. You will also want to estimate the number of hours faculty and staff spend on the hiring process. The cost of a mentoring program is likely to be less per mentee than the cost of the advertisement alone.

The third area of assessment is determining the state of mentoring on campus. Do some departments do a good job, while others do some initial orientation but no other mentoring, and others have no formal program at all? You can assess this through a faculty survey or a series of focus groups. Appendix I contains a sample survey of mentoring practices on campus (p. 119).

Determine Campus Resources

Now you will need to look at the various campus resources from the perspective of what would serve the needs of new faculty. Adding these to your proposal will demonstrate to the administration that the program can use current resources to reduce costs. There are obvious resources in the Teaching and Learning Center, the Office of Community Engagement, and the Office of Research, though the last may be limited to help with grant writing. Talk with the director of the Writing Center about whether support is available for new faculty for whom English is a second language. If there is a Speech and Hearing Clinic, accent reduction services may be available. Determine whether there is a statistical consulting center on campus that new faculty can use. Sidebar 6.1 lists possible resources for new faculty members.

Another resource to pin down is appropriate meeting space(s) for group mentoring. Ideally it should not be a seminar room with a table in the center, but should be an informal space with comfortable chairs. If there is a table at the center, it should be low so that nothing blocks the space between people.

SIDEBAR 6.1

Potential resources for new faculty on campus

- Teaching and Learning Center
- Office of Research
- Statistical Consulting
- Writing Center
- Accent Reduction in Speech and Hearing Clinic
- Office of Community Engagement
- Editorial Writing Support
- Diversity Office

Third, you will want to recruit someone who is skilled in group facilitation to train the senior faculty members who will become group facilitators. Most faculty members tend to be introverts and do not find that group facilitation comes easily to them. Most campuses will have departments in which you can find people ideally suited to the task, such as social work, counseling, and communication studies.

Another resource that would be very helpful to new faculty is a cadre of experienced editors. Writing manuscripts for journals is very different from writing a dissertation, and even new faculty members with a few publications will have fragile competence in this area. It will be difficult to find faculty members with the time for this in their busy schedules, but you might consider recruiting retired faculty and alumni of your institution. If funds are available, the university can hire an academic professional editor.

If part of your program will be to provide web resources, then you will need to determine where your website or webpages will be hosted, and what other webpages should include a link to yours. You will also want a links page to campus resources such as those listed in Sidebar 6.1.

You initially will want to plan a website that provides information for new recruits, be they mentees or mentors. If your job will include departmental resources, you will find many possibilities in Appendix H that you can modify to meet the needs of your particular campus.

Pilot-Test the Program

You may find it beneficial to include a pilot year in your proposal. Many things can be learned in a pilot year, and you may need to make modifications to the model proposed here or elsewhere to best serve the needs on your campus. Early success of a new program can be crucial to maintaining support, so a built-in pilot year can prevent rectifiable difficulties from sinking the program in its infancy.

The proposal should include an initial assessment for the pilot year that is formative, so that issues that are raised during that year and the end-of-year assessment can be addressed in the following year. If, during the pilot year, you have a reduced budget and must leave out some aspects of the model program, you can use the assessment tools to determine the effects of doing without. An assessment after only one year will not give you any long-term data for many of the program's goals, but you might include a stress questionnaire along with the formative assessment questionnaire, which we discuss next.

Planning for Assessment

As with any proposal, you must indicate how you will know whether the program is successful. Some of your assessments should evaluate short-term goals, and others long-term goals. Table 6.1 shows an example of how you might outline your goals and assessments.

In addition, in the first year you might use focus groups in the spring semester in addition to a final survey. People in focus groups often generate richer and more in-depth information than a questionnaire as ideas may surface from one person that another had not considered, and may lead to new ideas being offered.

As you meet with mentors and group facilitators during the year, take careful notes. These meetings are wonderful for generating improvements to an existing program.

Implementation of a University-Wide Mentoring Program

Overview of a Model Program

We are describing a program in which new faculty in their first three years working at the university can participate. If you will be offering this program to nontenure-track and adjunct faculty, we highly recommend that the programs for tenure-track, nontenure-track, and adjunct faculty be separate, as each group of people will have very different needs. Each new faculty participant is paired with a mentor, a choice in which the mentee participates. New mentees are also placed in a mentoring group facilitated by two senior faculty members. Both the mentoring pair and the group meet once a month. Mentors and group facilitators also meet as a group once a month.

We have been fortunate as well in having support funds for a mini-grant for each mentee, for which they must write a one- to two-page proposal. Our good fortune has also included a small account for each mentor and group facilitator, which serves as a recruitment incentive and also binds their commitment to the work.

Recruiting Mentors, Group Facilitators, and Mentees

A good place to start recruiting mentors is by writing invitations to professors who have won teaching and

TABLE 6.1
Outline of Program Goals and Assessments

Short-Term Goals	Assessment	Long-Term Goals	Assessment
Make good matches	Early phone call	Retention of new faculty	5-year data from institutional research
Make connections across campus	Question on final survey	Productivity of new faculty	Post-program survey to former mentees
Create a 5-year plan	Question on final survey	Achievement of tenure	Post program survey or institutional data

research awards. The invitations can indicate that interested people can choose between one-on-one mentoring and group facilitation. Another possibility is asking the deans to recommend people as mentors. An e-mail from the dean to a recommended professor, with a copy to you, can work wonders in the early days of developing your cadre of mentors. Deans and department heads will probably want to be involved in screening applicants, so asking for a letter of intent from professors who are interested can be helpful. The letter of intent can include something about their research and teaching interests and any mentoring experience they may have. At our university, the deans and department heads sign off on the mentoring assignment, indicating that the mentor or group facilitator will receive credit for the work as university service.

Recruiting mentees must be done in the spring and involves determining which departments are currently conducting searches for new faculty. Although this could be done in the fall, you will lose the mentoring program as a recruitment tool for hiring the best new faculty possible. There will also be a loss of time, as recruitment will cut into the academic year, reducing the amount of support available. It can be difficult to determine if a hire is made, so recruitment materials should be sent to the chair of the search committee or the department head, to be sure they reach potential participants.

New faculty members often participate in the program in their second year on campus, and they find this arrangement to be very satisfactory. We have had success recruiting these people by sending a personal letter of invitation indicating the benefits of participating in the program. It should be possible to obtain a list of actual new hires from the new faculty orientation list of the previous year.

New faculty participants complete an application form, an example of which is in Appendix F (p. 88). This will give you demographic information as well as research and teaching interests and needs. You will find it helpful to begin the very first year by constructing a database of this information to which you can refer when someone is looking for a collaborator on a teaching or research project. There is a sign-off sheet included (p. 91), to be sure their department head and dean are aware of their participation in the program.

Training Mentors and Group Facilitators

Training mentors and group facilitators new to the program can be accomplished in a half-day workshop (see "Mentor Training Agenda for a Three-Hour Session," Appendix I, p. 120). Ongoing questions and issues can be addressed in the monthly meetings of each. Some aspects of the training are similar for both groups, and can be found in chapter 2 for mentors:

- typical characteristics of new faculty;
- common pitfalls of new faculty; and
- characteristics of quick starters.

Training for mentors will also include a discussion of the characteristics of good mentors, with an emphasis on the fact that there is no one good way to mentor. You will want to discuss the needs of new faculty, and that personality differences will mean that some faculty members (both new and experienced) are more comfortable with a strictly work/accomplishment-driven style, while others will want a more relaxed, supportive style that includes work/life balance issues. It will be helpful to provide mentors with ideas for areas in which they can help their mentees; these are included as various worksheets in Appendix C. In Appendix F you will find an outline of a short version of a mentor orientation tailored for mentors who have participated in previous years (p. 93).

You will want to discuss diversity issues, as research shows that new faculty prefer to be mentored by someone who looks like them (Okawa, 2002; Patton, 2009; Welch, 1996). It is entirely possible that you will find yourself with a cadre of mentors and mentees that will not match up on that basis. Good professional mentoring can still occur, although psychosocial needs may not be met in such a pair. This is one of the reasons group mentoring is a good complement to one-on-one mentoring; it can provide for psychosocial needs and peer support. If you are able to provide a full-day training program, you can include diversity training, using the resources from the Office of Diversity and Inclusion on your campus. You also may want to provide an introduction to the various worksheets participants may use, or introduce them individually at the monthly meetings as the year progresses.

Training for group facilitators is very important. Most faculty members have some experience with one-on-one mentoring, but very few have experience facilitating a good group experience. Chapter 2 has step-by-step instructions for implementing a group mentoring program.

Opening Activities

The academic year opens with a meet-and-greet event, but before that, it is a good idea to provide an orientation to the program for the new mentees (see "New Faculty Mentoring Program Mentee Orientation," Appendix F, p. 95). Much of the same material used in training the mentors can be used here, as new faculty often recognize themselves in the descriptions of typical new faculty and will benefit from hearing about the common pitfalls. The same list of areas in which mentors can help new faculty can be shared with the mentees. It is important to convey at this orientation what they can expect from the mentoring relationship, and that it will not be with someone from their department who can help them with their research and coauthor papers with them. Last, you will want to describe how the meet-and-greet will function and what the mentees might do to prepare for this event. If you have a website, it is very helpful to have a page introducing the mentors with a photo and short biography of each for the mentees to read before the event.

We have found that the most effective and efficient way for all of the mentees to meet the mentors is to have a five-minute meet, which is the central focus of the opening event. It is helpful to provide a worksheet for the mentees with photos of the mentors and space for notes beside or beneath the photo. Second- and third-year mentees report that they received more mentoring in each of those five-minute sessions than they did since they arrived on the job. The purpose of the meet is to find someone with whom they feel a rapport. Afterward the mentees will provide you with a list of three to five mentors with whom they feel they could work well, and you will sort out the matches. This event is a good time to have all participants sign a statement of commitment and confidentiality, found on page 97 in Appendix F.

Monthly Meetings With Group Facilitators and Mentors

The director can use the mentor and group facilitator learning communities as an opportunity to share leadership. The senior faculty members who participate in the program are there because they want to help new faculty, and this means they have ideas about how to do so based on their own experience. Sharing those ideas with one another gives everyone a fuller picture of what mentees need. Issues that may be pertinent to your campus will come up and can be addressed. In some cases, the mentors in the program can be advocates with the administration for needs of new faculty. The director should attempt to create groups of six to eight mentors to have effective conversations.

These meetings of small groups of mentors and group facilitators start with the same brief go-around exercise that allows us to get to know one another better. What did you do over break? What teacher or professor inspired you? What great thing happened this past month? This is followed by another go-around in which the mentors talk about how the mentoring relationship is going this month. Often, particularly in the beginning, they talk about a problem a mentee is having, describing how they advised their mentee and asking if others have any ideas. The combined wisdom in the room is brought to bear on the issue. This go-around is also an informal method of accountability to check whether the mentors are actually meeting with their mentees. This is a good place for the director to share other resources for working with mentees, found in Appendix H, such as a five-year tenure plan (p. 117) and possible tasks to assign to a graduate assistant (p. 111).

The leadership sharing part of the meeting revolves around a general question about the life of a university professor. What are the tenure requirements in your department? Are new professors protected from onerous service assignments? How do you maintain balance in your life? Together we are building a picture of what kind of support new professors need. The director will share with them what needs have arisen in the new faculty learning communities and were shared by the group facilitators. The director can also give feedback by sharing general results from early assessments of the program. Sometimes ideas come up in one mentor group meeting that are shared to spark discussion of an issue in another mentor group meeting. It is important to discuss the same issues in more than one mentor learning community as the results can be very different from group to group. Getting the viewpoint of only one group can result in a skewed interpretation.

Closing Out the Year

Before the academic year is over, a questionnaire assessment should be sent to all participants. If you intend to use the collated results from these assessments in presentations or publications, then you should prepare and have approved an Institutional Review Board (IRB) application. If you will use these surveys only in a formative manner to improve the program and for annual reporting, an IRB application is not necessary. A sample assessment can be found on page 100 in Appendix G.

Quotations from the final evaluations can be used in an annual newsletter, which can be included in recruitment materials, sent to deans and department heads, and posted on the website. Other information for the newsletter might be a page introducing the mentees who participated this year and an article on what kinds of research/teaching projects the minigrants supported. A short follow-up questionnaire will allow you to include updates on former mentees (for example, see "New Faculty Mentoring Program Follow-up Questionnaire," Appendix G, p. 105).

An event to bring together all participants will provide a nice closure to the year. One possibility is a picnic to which the mentees' families can be invited. Often there are very few, if any, events on campus that families can participate in, so young faculty members appreciate such an event. As the program continues, participants from previous years can also be invited, and can provide more opportunities for new faculty to make connections across campus.

References

Okawa, G. (2002). Diving for pearls: Mentoring relationships among African American women in graduate and professional schools. *College Composition and Communication, 53*(3), 507–532.

Patton, L. (2009). My sister's keeper: A qualitative examination of mentoring experiences among African American women in graduate and professional schools. *Journal of Higher Education, 80*(5), 510–537.

Phillips, S. L., Crane, P., & Dennison, S. T. (2010). Establishing a new faculty mentoring program: Proposal development. *Journal on Centers for Teaching and Learning, 2*, 37–51.

Welch, O. (1996). *An examination of effective mentoring models in the academy.* Paper presented at the Annual Meeting of the American Educational Research Association (New York City, April 8–13, 1996). EDRS ED394464 HE 029160

CHAPTER 7

Review of Mentoring in the Higher Education Literature

In this chapter we provide major points surfacing from the literature on formalized mentoring both in regard to inter- and intradepartmental mentoring and university-wide mentoring programs. We have limited this literature review to (a) the importance or value of new faculty mentoring; (b) logistics related to effectively setting up, maintaining, evaluating, and sustaining faculty mentoring programs; (c) the benefits of these relationships; and (d) the challenges of mentoring programs. The intent of this targeted review of the related literature is to provide research/studies that further validate material provided in this book.

It is important, before you review this literature, to keep in mind that most of the systematic studies on more formal mentoring programs have been reported only since the early 1990s, with most articles before that decade being descriptive in nature (Merriam, Thomas, & Zeph, 1987). Wunsch (1994) noted even in the mid-1990s that research on mentoring in higher education was "rare and fraught with methodological pitfalls" (p. 32). One of the few and earliest studies in the academy that examined the nature and extent to which faculty mentor other faculty was conducted by Sands, Parson, and Duane (1991). Data for this latter study were based on a survey of faculty at a public research-oriented university in the Midwest. Sands et al. (1991) concluded that "mentorship is a complex, multidimensional activity" (p. 189) with their research identifying four types of mentors (friend, career guide, information source, and intellectual guide). However, more recent researchers have divided the role of mentor into four subsidiary roles of sponsor, coach, role model, and counselor, and these are seen as more

collective functions (Clutterbuck & Lane, 2004; Daloz, 1999; Luecke, 2004; Murray, 2001).

Another controversial issue in this literature is the lack of consensus on a definition of *mentoring* (Zellers, Howard, & Barcie, 2008). Some researchers like Clutterbuck and Lane (2004) have noted that much of the mentoring literature is invalidated because it is not clear what types of relationships are being studied, while other studies (Angelique, Kyle, & Taylor, 2002; Cawyer, Simonds, & Davis, 2002) have put mentoring experiences on a continuum. Clutterbuck and Lane (2004) also point out in their research that "to some extent, definitions do not matter greatly, if those in the role of mentor and mentee have a clear and mutual understanding of what is expected of them and what they should in turn expect of their mentoring partner" (p. xvi).

The Value and Importance of Faculty Mentoring

Many personal benefits of formal mentoring are reported in the literature (which we address later in this chapter), but these findings are somewhat different from the institutional or departmental benefits of this new faculty supportive strategy. Rather, these are factors that are significantly influencing or driving higher education to consider investing in faculty mentoring programs. There appear to be four commonly shared needs causing many colleges/universities to consider formal mentoring programs today. These needs include (a) recruitment of a high-quality, diverse faculty; (b) retention of high-quality, diverse faculty; (c) economic savings and benefits for the institution; and (d) preservation of the mission, culture, and norms of a particular higher education setting. This part of the literature review specifically addresses these four needs, which more clearly point out and identify the importance of mentoring to universities' current and future challenges.

The business field has a much longer history of recognizing the importance of mentoring for recruitment and retention of employees, which significantly helps companies maintain a completive advantage (Kanter, 1977). However, higher education settings are now finding that they are experiencing a new generation of junior faculty who are more likely to be women, minorities, and foreign nationals (Collins, Slough, & Waxman, 2009; Zafar, Roberts, & Behar-Harenstein, 2012). Furthermore, there is a need to find quality replacement faculty as a generation of baby boomers is retiring from the academy over the next several years (Clayton, 2007). In addition, colleges and universities are finding that this new generation of academics is increasingly reporting feelings of marginalization and exclusion from more informal mentoring (Boyle & Boice, 1998; Darwin & Palmer, 2009; Ragines & Cotton, 1999). So it is not surprising that recruitment and retention of high-quality, diverse faculty members are the first two most important ways that mentoring programs can prove beneficial and critical to a higher education institution's ability to compete successfully in the future.

The third factor that could influence higher education to consider investing in formal mentoring programs has been related to economics, both in cost savings when faculty turnover is lower (Kreitner & Kinicki, 2004; Luecke, 2004) and in increased funding for important research (Steiner, Lamphear, Curtis, & Vu, 2002; Zahorski, 2002). The university's investment in new faculty members today is extensive, including but not limited to advertising for recruitment, interviewing costs, orientation, start-up costs for some areas of research, and, in some cases, reduced teaching loads until faculty have attained tenure. Detmar (2004) has this to say about the estimated costs of hiring a new professor:

My rough calculations suggest that when one factors in the cost of advertising a position; of the time spent by search-committee members, support staff, and college and university administrators in reviewing letters of application, curricula vitae, letters of recommendation, and writing samples; of sending the search committee to a national conference for initial screening; and of bringing finalists to the campus for interviews, the price of conducting a tenure-track search is about the same as the first-year salary of that new faculty member (at least in the humanities). (p. B8)

There is also increased pressure today on new faculty members to secure external funding for their research that is often now part of the requirements for achieving tenure at some institutions (Darwin & Palmer, 2009). Formal mentoring programs address this issue as educational settings find that institutions with such programs report increased research income and publication rates (Gardiner, 2005). Collins et al. (2009) indicate that one of the reasons junior faculty today are not as productive in their research or acquisition of external funding as faculty have been in the past is more related to the lack of opportunities to engage in collaborative work with senior faculty, which has resulted in excellent examples of apprenticeships. Many of these new faculty members have learned the knowledge necessary to conduct their research and write their related manuscripts in their doctoral programs; however, they often benefit greatly from the experience, resource information, and guidance of more seasoned faculty members.

The fourth value of mentoring to higher education is the need to have new faculty members assimilate more rapidly into an institution's mission, culture, structure, and norms (Luna & Cullen, 1995; Murray, 2001). Higher education, similar to other institutions today, is facing many new pressures that are threatening to change how universities will run their operations in the future. Some of these pressures include budget reductions (which in some states has involved serious reductions in yearly budgets), shifts in how politicians view the primary mission of universities/colleges, and student loan funding changes. As a result, higher education settings must be more intentional in their efforts to safeguard what they consider as their primary mission, culture, and norms (Brint, Proctor, Mulligan, Rotondi, & Hanneman, 2012; Doyle, 2012). Historically, the academy has been dependent on its senior faculty to continue indoctrinating the next generation of faculty on the mission, culture, and norms of a particular institution (Bergquist, 1991; Sorcinelli, 2000). Formal faculty mentoring programs not only address this need to assimilate new faculty more efficiently into a university's mission and related goals but also to improve leadership capacity among its faculty, allowing for succession planning (Jossi, 1997; Murray, 2001). Moreover, agencies like the U.S. Department of Health and Human Services Office of Research Integrity recognize mentoring as an essential way for institutions to foster responsible conduct among future generations of scientists (Steneck, 2004). And last but not least, formal mentoring programs where new faculty are able to work with good mentors can benefit a higher education institution by reinforcing the legacy of mentoring within that setting (Cho, Ramanan, & Feldman, 2011).

Logistics Related to Successful Mentoring Programs

In this section of the literature review, we provide related research and, in some cases, reported program descriptions that indicate several logistical issues that a department and/or university needs to consider and plan before it begins a new faculty mentoring program. These operational factors include (a) the need for administrative support and possible related policies; (b) the determination of clear goals and objectives for the program; (c) identification of who will oversee/coordinate the program; (d) the decision whether to have individual and/or group mentoring; (e) the procedure used to match mentees with mentors; (f) potential funding for both mentees and mentors; (g) strategies for providing service recognition or other rewards to mentors; (h) specific training of mentors and/or facilitators of groups; (i) length of time mentors are assigned to mentees; (j) frequency of individual and/or group sessions; (k) the determination of an

evaluation design; and (l) a plan for sustainability of the program.

The literature has reported a plethora of program characteristics and best practices for faculty mentoring programs (Boice, 1992; Johnson, 2007; Johnson & Riley, 2008; Luna & Cullen, 1995; Nakamura, Shenoff, & Hooker, 2009). Regardless of the type of mentoring program being planned (interdepartmental, intradepartmental, or university-wide) there is a need to elicit support at the administrative level before initiating a formal mentoring program (Boyle & Boice, 1998; Phillips, Crane, & Dennison, 2010; Tahtinen, Mainela, Natti, & Saraniemi, 2012). Eliciting such administrative support can involve anything from a meeting with a relevant administrator to provide knowledge about the purpose and goals of such a program to having a full advisory committee work with departmental, school, or university administrators to formulate a policy on such a practice, along with specific related procedures (Boyle & Boice, 1998; Lumpkin, 2011; Phillips et al., 2010; Wunsch, 1994). Sometimes one way to begin this step is to identify how a mentoring program is related to the department and/or university's mission statement and/or strategic plan (Phillips et al., 2010).

Someone, or a committee of faculty members and/or administrators, should determine clearly the purpose and measurable goals for such a mentoring program, along with operational strategies, before trying to secure stakeholders' support (Boyle & Boice, 1998; Lumpkin, 2011; Phillips et al., 2010). By ensuring administrative support for the program before it begins, the involved administrators will be more likely to provide release time for a coordinator, meeting space, and, potentially, various forms of financial support (Boyle & Boice, 1998; Phillips et al., 2010; Wunsch, 1994).

Overseeing or coordinating a mentoring program can be done by one faculty member as part of his or her position, or it can be done by a designated coordinator who has been given teaching release time to carry out such duties. Determining the best way to handle this role will depend on the type of mentoring program being planned (inter-/intradepartmental or university-wide) and available faculty time to take on such a role (Phillips et al., 2010). Often interdepartmental and intradepartmental mentoring programs are handled either by the involved departmental chairs or an assigned senior faculty member (Borders et al., 2011; Lumpkin, 2011). University-wide programs typically will require more time to oversee; they are often facilitated by either a designated coordinator or director (Phillips et al., 2010).

Mentoring programs in higher education traditionally have involved individual mentoring. However, in the past decade some research has addressed the value of either adding a mentoring group/circle to individual mentorship or providing only this format for mentoring (Cook, 2005; Cox, 2001; Darwin, 2000; Darwin & Palmer, 2009; Moss, Teshima, & Leszcz, 2008; Phillips et al., 2010). Boyle and Boice (1998) reported that some of the best mentoring programs included weekly meetings with individual mentors, weekly ratings of mentor interactions, and monthly group sessions. These groups have been (a) peer groups that do not have a senior faculty facilitator and (b) mentoring groups that are facilitated by one or more senior faculty members (Zellers et al., 2008). "Both peer and group mentoring are formats that have the potential to provide women, non-White men, and other minorities with access to same-culture mentoring in environments in which White men represent the majority" (Zellers et al., 2008, p. 565). In addition, one of the major benefits that junior faculty report from mentoring circles is that they feel less isolated and more connected to others on the campus (Darwin & Palmer, 2009; Phillips et al., 2010).

The next four operational factors the literature addresses relate to the mentees and mentors and include matching mentees with mentors, funding faculty in these relationships, service recognition strategies for mentors, and training mentors. There have been numerous articles written about how to match mentors with mentees (Allen, Elby, & Lentz, 2006; Boyle & Boice, 1998; Tillman, 2001; Wilson, Valentine, & Pereira, 2002). Both Welch (1996) and Okawa (2002) discovered that African American women found it very helpful to be paired with someone of the same identity group, even though this was not the only important factor for ensuring the effectiveness of

these relationships. In addition, many researchers have found that female faculty members feel more comfortable having a female mentor and are more appreciative of these relationships (Patton, 2009). Although selecting a mentor from a group of potential senior faculty can be uncomfortable for a junior faculty member, studies have found that mentee input in this decision usually increases the chances of successful mentoring relationships (Allen et al., 2006; Bell & Treleaven, 2011; Wilson et al., 2002).

Since the mid-1990s, the literature has focused more on the senior faculty members who serve in mentoring roles. It seems that the longer universities have had formal mentoring programs, the needs of these individuals have become more apparent. It does appear that many researchers have found intrinsic reasons why senior faculty members are willing to serve as mentors. For example, some mentors report a sense of contribution (Murray, 2001), personal satisfaction (Johnson-Bailey & Cervero, 2004), and personal development (Beans, 1999; Murray, 2001). However, more recent literature has pointed out the need to elicit upper administration support for providing university recognition to senior faculty members who serve in these roles (Phillips et al., 2010). Some authors have discussed the value of offering stipends to mentors (Boyle & Boice, 1998), while others have suggested release time for mentees as a form of reinforcement for participating in mentoring (Wingard, Garman, & Reznik, 2004). In addition, authors have discussed the need to provide professional development to mentors (Allen et al., 2006; Cox, 1997), with particular emphasis on enhancing the cultural competency among White male mentors who often are the only senior faculty to mentor new minority faculty members (Johnson-Bailey & Cervero, 2004). For example, Stanley (2006) points out that faculty of color often are more overburdened with committee work and having to advise larger numbers of students, particularly students of color. Turner (2006) also points out that faculty of color are often more challenged in the classroom by students.

The next set of operational issues involves the length of time for mentoring assignments/matches and the frequency of meetings. "To maximize the potential benefits for protégés and mentors, spending time together is imperative" (Lumpkin, 2011, p. 359). Boyle and Boice (1998) suggest that one-on-one mentoring ideally should take place weekly and group mentoring at least once a month. Furthermore, Cox (1997) recommends that all scheduled mentoring meetings be monitored, by the person overseeing the mentoring program or assigned within a department, until they become routine.

The next logistical issue involved the evaluation design used to determine the outcomes of either inter-/intradepartmental or university-wide mentoring programs. Both formative and summative evaluations should be conducted on these programs so that the director or coordinator of the mentoring program is checking regularly to see how these relationships are developing and, at the end, will be able to see the program's major positive outcomes and problems (Lumpkin, 2011). Unfortunately, Zellers et al.'s (2008) "review of the academic literature reveals that studies of formal faculty mentoring program that use research designs and include descriptions of mentoring program models continue to be rare" (p. 568). In fact, Zellers et al. (2008) identified only seven studies between 1994 and 2004 that met the criteria. In her review of the mentoring literature, Lumpkin (2011) suggests that "one way to measure the effectiveness of mentoring is to directly obtain qualitative feedback from protégés and mentors" (p. 374). Mertens (2005) made this same point earlier when he indicated that qualitative methods are better suited to examine the effectiveness of the complexity of mentoring relationships.

The last operational factor that departments and/or universities should include when planning a mentoring program is that supports are in place that will ensure the sustainability of the program even after key faculty or administrators leave the institution. Girves, Zepeda, and Gwathmey (2005) discussed the difficulty of institutionalizing and sustaining mentoring programs at the university/college level, which any of the related literature rarely discusses. The mentoring programs the Zellers et al. (2008) review cited, with the exception of one program, were all supported by federal grants. So the question remains: What happens to these programs once those federal funds run out?

As Zellers et al. (2008) so clearly point out, "Strategies to compel senior administrators to invest internal resources in more robust studies of faculty mentoring programs would advance our understanding of the both the power and perils of such programs" (p. 583).

Benefits of Mentoring Programs

The literature reports a number of benefits resulting from formal mentoring programs in higher education. These benefits appear to fall into three categories: benefits for the institution, benefits for the mentees, and benefits for the mentors. We mentioned some of the benefits for the university earlier in this chapter, particularly in regard to recruitment and retention of minority faculty (Ambrose, Huston, & Norman, 2005; Detmar, 2004). These programs often can assist an institution in initiating strategies not only for recruiting diverse faculty, but also as a way to make a university more inclusive and to ensure that faculty mentoring is available more consistently across the various units on any one campus (Phillips et al., 2010). Mullen and Hutinger (2008) indicate in their empirical case study that mentoring can help a university move "beyond the goal of effectiveness to cultural change, faculty mentoring programs can help to reculture organizations" (p. 200). In other words, these programs can assist entire institutions to become learning organizations where mentoring is practiced widely (Gladwell, 2002). Mentoring programs are also very effective ways to help new faculty assimilate into the culture, mission, and goals of an institution (Mullen & Hutinger, 2008; Otieno, Lutz, & Schoolmaster, 2010).

The literature has reported a wide range of benefits for individual mentees in relation to both their one-on-one mentoring and group mentoring experiences. For example, these programs can assist faculty of color in addressing some of the unique challenges they face in predominantly White institutions where they often have to deal with challenges from students in the classroom, devaluation of their research efforts, and being asked to do more university service work (Thompson, 2008). Aguirre (2000) notes: "Mentoring activities can alter the academic culture's response to the inclusion of minorities in academe" (p. 80). In addition, junior faculty who participate in these programs are more productive scholars, more confident teachers, and report higher career satisfaction (de Janasz & Sullivan, 2004; Lucas & Murray, 2002). Moreover, mentoring programs have been found to enhance junior faculty members' teaching skills (Beckerman, 2010; Boyle & Boyce, 1998), online course development and instruction (Hixon, Barczyk, Buckenmeyer, & Feldman, 2011), and research competencies (Johnston & McComack, 1997; Zahorski, 2002).

For those junior faculty who participate in formal group mentoring programs, some additional, and often unique, benefits are reported. First and foremost, mentoring in higher education addresses the social isolation that new faculty often report as part of this working environment (Christman, 2003; Stanley, 2006). This mentoring format is more likely to provide women and minority faculty access to same-culture mentoring, which is very important in many institutions whose faculties comprise mostly White men (Zellers et al., 2008). Furthermore, these groups provide junior faculty with more interactions between departments and thus more relationship building across a campus (Cook, 2005; Spencer, 2005; West, 2004). By supporting these mentoring groups, universities encourage more clearly and consistently the need for more collaboration between faculty members and disciplines (Darwin & Palmer, 2009).

The literature also identifies many benefits that senior faculty members who have served as mentors have reported. Some have said that this experience has provided a sense of accomplishment (Fogg, 2003) and personal satisfaction (Johnson-Bailey & Cervero, 2004). In addition, they have noted a renewed interest in their own work (Jossi, 1997; Murray, 2001), opportunities to hear new ideas (Beans, 1999), and new perspectives (Murray, 2001). Mentors have also reported greater productivity in their research efforts, more networking across their campus, and enhanced sense of professional accomplishment as their mentees do well (Johnson, 2002).

Challenges of Mentoring Programs

As we have noted, many benefits have been reported in the literature for higher education settings, for junior faculty who elect to be involved in mentoring, and for those senior faculty members who serve as mentors. However, this same literature has reported some challenges as well. Because women and minority faculty are in short supply in senior faculty roles across most campuses today, it is very difficult, even in university-wide mentoring programs, to provide same-culture mentoring (Zellers et al., 2008). This is especially true in the sciences and even across all disciplines, as West and Curtis (2006) have found that in 2003 women only occupied 24% of all full-professor positions. One of the challenges for cross-race mentoring relationships is what Thomas (2001, p. 105) calls "protective hesitation," which means that both parties avoid discussing particularly sensitive issues. This point leads into the next challenge, which is the need to train mentors so they are better prepared for these roles (Cox, 1997), including, in some cases, cultural competency training (Johnson-Bailey & Cervero, 2004).

Matching mentors with mentees can also be challenging, particularly when mentoring is done within a department since pairing in mentoring should be avoided if the mentor has any evaluative authority or supervisory role over the mentee (Zellers et al., 2008). For this reason, Boyle and Boice (1998) suggest that cross-department pairing is less political than intradepartmental mentoring. Another challenge relates to the need to have regularly scheduled meeting times for the one-on-one mentoring and/or group, which are essential if the mentee is to benefit from this experience (Cox, 1997). The difficulty is that some mentor pairs may not keep to a schedule for various reasons. This is why it is often necessary to have a designated person who, in the beginning months, monitors these mentoring meeting times (Lumpkin, 2011).

Because there continues to be a shortage of women and minority faculty in senior faculty positions at most universities, another challenge is the shortage of these individuals to serve as mentors. Some of the challenges related to the cross-gender pairings include a greater likelihood of the relationship becoming paternalistic

(Christman, 2003), pairs that are less likely to engage in outside social activities (Luecke, 2004), and male mentors who can be less inclined to talk with mentees about their psychosocial needs, which has been found to be more important to women (McCauley & Van Velsor, 2004). When following a departmental or school-wide mentoring format, establishing mentoring pairs between departments may be one way to address and avoid these challenges.

Another major challenge for mentoring programs is evaluation of the outcomes of these efforts. As Zellers et al. (2008) found, there are very few well-designed research studies of mentoring in higher education, thus resulting in a lack of scholarship. One of the reasons why there are so very few rigorous studies is that the people overseeing or coordinating mentoring programs are fulfilling this role as their university service, so they do not have enough time to devote to this type of evaluation (Zellers et al., 2008). This issue is directly related to the last major challenge for mentoring in higher education. When Zellers et al. (2008) conducted their review of the literature, other than one study, all other research reported involved a program that was being funded by a federal grant. The question is, What happens to these mentoring programs once that grant money runs out? As Phillips et al. (2010) suggest, it may be wise for universities to design and plan these programs as part of another structure on the campus, which would also ensure ongoing funding. This sustainability issue is a real concern, particularly in the current economic climate.

References

Aguirre, A. (2000). *Issues facing women and minority faculty. Women and minority faculty in the academic workplace: Recruitment and retention, and academic culture.* San Francisco: Jossey-Bass.

Allen, T., Elby, L., & Lentz, E. (2006). Mentorship behaviors and mentorship quality associated with formal mentoring programs: Closing the gap between research and practice. *Journal of Applied Psychology, 9*(3), 567–578.

Ambrose, S., Huston, T., & Norman, M. (2005). A qualitative method for assessing faculty satisfaction. *Research in Higher Education, 46*(7), 803–830.

Angelique, H., Kyle, K., & Taylor, E. (2002). Mentors and muses: New strategies for academic success. *Innovative Higher Education, 26*(3), 195–209.

Beans, B. (1999). Mentoring program helps young faculty feel at home. *APA Monitor Online, 30*(3). Retrieved May 18, 2013, from http://www.apa.org/monitor/mar99/mentor.html

Beckerman, N. (2010). Teaching teachers. *Academe, 96*(4), 28–29.

Bell, A., & Treleaven, L. (2011). Looking for professor right: Mentee selection of mentors in a formal mentoring program. *Higher Education, 61*(5), 545–561.

Bergquist, W. (1991). *The four cultures of the academy.* San Francisco: Jossey-Bass.

Boice, R. (1992). *The new faculty member.* San Francisco: Jossey-Bass.

Borders, L., Young, S., Wester, K., Murray, C., Villalba, J., Lewis, T., & Mobley, A. (2011). Mentoring promotion/tenure-seeking faculty: Principles of good practice within a counselor education program. *Counselor Education & Supervision, 50,* 171–188.

Boyle, P., & Boice, B. (1998). Systematic mentoring for new faculty teachers and graduate teaching assistants. *Innovative Higher Education, 22*(4), 157–179.

Brint, S., Proctor, K., Mulligan, D., Rotondi, M., & Hanneman, R. (2012). Declining academic fields in U.S. four-year college and universities, 1970–2006. *Journal of Higher Education, 84*(4), 582–613.

Cawyer, C., Simonds, C., & Davis, S. (2002). Mentoring to facilitate socialization: The case of the new faculty member. *Qualitative Studies in Education, 15*(2), 225–242.

Christman, D. (2003). Women faculty in higher education: Impeded by academe. *Advancing Women in Leadership Online Journal, 14.*

Cho, C., Ramana, R., & Feldman, M. (2011). Defining the ideal qualities of mentorship: A qualitative analysis of the characteristics of outstanding mentors. *The American Journal of Medicine, 124*(5), 453–458.

Clayton, C. (2007). Curriculum making as novice professional development: Practice risk taking learning in high stakes times. *Journal of Teacher Education, 58*(3), 216–230.

Clutterbuck, D., & Lane, G. (Eds.). (2004). *The situational mentor: An international review of competencies and capabilities in mentoring.* Burlington, VT: Gower.

Collins, T., Slough, S., & Waxman, H. (2009). Lesson learned about mentoring junior faculty in higher education. *Academic Leadership, 7*(2), 1–5.

Cook, A. (2005). Mentoring circles: Workshop Presentation at Colorado State University. Retrieved May 18, 2013, from http://cfw.utk.edu/mentoring_circles.html

Cox, M. (1997). Long-term patterns in a mentoring program for junior faculty: Recommendations for practice. In D. Dezure & M. Kaplan (Eds.), *To improve the academy, 16,* 225–268. Stillwater, OK: Forum Press and the Professional and Organizational Development Network in Higher Education.

Cox, M. D. (2001). Faculty learning communities: Change agents for transforming institutions into learning organizations. *To Improve the Academy, 19,* 69–93.

Daloz, L. (1999). *Mentor: Guiding the journey of adult learners.* San Francisco: Jossey-Bass.

Darwin, A. (2000). Critical reflections on mentoring in work settings. *Adult Education Quarterly, 50*(3), 197–211.

Darwin, A., & Palmer, E. (2009). Mentoring circles in higher education. *Higher Education Research and Development, 28*(2), 125–136.

de Janasz, S., & Sullivan, S. (2004). Multiple mentoring in academe: Developing the professional network. *Journal of Vocational Behavior, 64,* 263–283.

Detmar, K. (2004). What we waste when faculty hiring goes wrong. *The Chronicle of Higher Education, 51*(17), 86–88.

Doyle, W. (2012). The politics of public college tuition and state financial aid. *Journal of Higher Education, 83*(5), 617–647.

Fogg, P. (2003). So many committees, so little time. *Chronicle of Higher Education, 50*(17), A14.

Gardiner, M. (2005). *Making a difference: Flinders University mentoring scheme for early career women researchers.* Adelaide: The Flinders University, Australia, Staff Development and Training Unit.

Girves, J., Zepeda, Y., & Gwathmey, J. (2005). Mentoring in a post-affirmative action world. *Journal of Social Issues, 61*(3), 449–479.

Gladwell, M. (2002). *The tipping point: How little things can make a big difference.* New York: Little, Brown, and Company.

Hixon, E., Barczyk, C., Buckenmeyer, J., & Feldman, L. (2011). Mentoring university faculty to become high quality online educators: A program evaluation. *Online Journal of Distance Learning Administration, 14*(4).

Johnson, B. (2002). The intentional mentor: Strategies and guidelines for the practice of mentoring. *Professional Psychology: Research and Practice, 33*(1), 88–96.

Johnson, W. (2007). *On being a mentor: A guide for higher education faculty.* Mahwah: NJ: Lawrence Erlbaum.

Johnson, W., & Riley, C. (2008). *The elements of mentoring.* (2nd ed.). New York: Palgrave Macmillan.

Johnson-Bailey, J., & Cervero, R. (2004). Mentoring in Black and White: The intricacies of cross-cultural mentoring. *Mentoring and Tutoring, 12*(1), 7–21.

Johnston, S., & McCormack, C. (1997). Developing research potential through a structured mentoring program: Issues arising. *Higher Education, 33,* 257–264.

Jossi, F. (1997). Mentoring in changing times. *Training and Development, 51*(8), 50–54.

Kanter, R. (1977). *Men and women of the corporation.* New York: Basic Books.

Kreitner, R., & Kinicki, A. (2004). *Organizational behavior* (6th ed.). New York: McGraw-Hill/Irwin.

Lucas, C., & Murray, J. (2002). *New faculty: A practical guide for academic beginners.* New York: Palgrave.

Luecke, R. (2004). *Coaching and mentoring: How to develop top talent and achieve stronger performance.* Boston: Harvard Business School Press.

Lumpkin, A. (2011). A model for mentoring university faculty. *Educational Forum, 75*(4), 357–368.

Luna, G., & Cullen, D. (1995). *Empowering the faculty: Mentoring redirected and renewed.* Washington, DC: George Washington University, Graduate School of Education and Human Development.

McCauley, C., & Van Velsor, E. (Eds.). (2004). *The Center for Creative Leadership handbook of leadership development* (2nd ed.). San Francisco: Jossey-Bass.

Merriam, S., Thomas, R., & Zeph, C. (1987). Mentoring in higher education: What we know now. *Review of Higher Educations, 1*(2), 199–210.

Mertens, D. (2005). *Research and evaluation n education and psychology: Integrating diversity with quantitative, qualitative, and mixed methods* (2nd ed.). Thousand Oaks, CA: Sage.

Moss, J., Teshima, J., & Leszcz, M. (2008). Peer group mentoring of junior faculty. *Academic Psychiatry, 32*(3), 230–235.

Mullen, C., & Hutinger, J. (2008). At the tipping point? Role of formal faculty mentoring in changing university research cultures. *Journal of In-Service Education, 34*(2), 181–204.

Murray, M. (2001). *Beyond the myths and magic of mentoring: How to facilitate an effective mentoring process.* San Francisco: Jossey-Bass.

Nakamura, J., Shenoff, J., & Hooker, C. (2009). *Good mentoring: Fostering excellent practice in higher education.* San Francisco: Jossey-Bass.

Okawa, G. (2002). Diving for pearls: Mentoring relationships among African American women in graduate and professional schools. *College Composition and Communication, 53*(3), 507–532.

Otieno, T., Lutz, P., & Schoolmaster, F. (2010). Enhancing recruitment, professional development, and socialization of junior faculty through formal mentoring programs. *Metropolitan Universities, 21*(2), 74–88.

Patton, L. (2009). My sister's keeper: A qualitative examination of mentoring experiences among African American women in graduate and professional schools. *Journal of Higher Education, 80*(5), 510–537.

Phillips, S., Crane, P., & Dennison, S. (2010). Establishing a new faculty mentoring program: Proposal development. *Journal of Centers for Teaching & Learning, 2,* 37–51.

Ragines, B., & Cotton, J. (1999). Mentor functions and outcomes: A comparison of men and women in formal and informal mentoring relationships. *Applied Psychology, 84*(4), 529–550.

Sands, R., Parson, A., & Duane, J. (1991). Faculty mentoring faculty in public university. *Journal of Higher Education, 62*(2), 174–193.

Sorcinelli, M. (2000). *Principles of good practice: Supporting early-career faculty.* Washington DC: American Association for Higher Education.

Spencer, C. (2005). *Mentoring made easy: A practical guide.* Retrieved May 18, 2013, from http://www.dpc.nsw.ogv.au/public_employment/working_in_nsw_public_sector/mentoring_made_easy_a_practice_guide_3rd_edition

Stanley, C. (2006). Summary and key recommendations for the recruitment and retention of faculty of color. In C. Stanley (ed.), *Faculty of color: Teaching in predominantly White colleges and universities* (pp. 361–368). Bolton, MA: Anker.

Steneck, N. (2004). *Introduction to the responsible conduct of research.* Washington, DC: U.S. Government Printing Office.

Steiner, J., Lamphear, B., Curtis, P., & Vu, K. (2002). Indicators of early research productivity among primary care fellows. *Journal of General Internal Medicine, 17,* 854–860.

Tahtinen, J., Mainela, T., Natti, S., & Saraniemi, S. (2012). Intradepartmental faculty mentoring in teaching marketing. *Journal of Marketing Education, 34*(1), 5–18.

Thomas, D. (2001). The truth about mentoring minorities: Race matters. *Harvard Business Review, 79,* 99–107.

Thompson, C. (2008). Recruitment, retention, and mentoring faculty of color: The chronicle continues. *New Directions for Higher Education, 143,* 47–54.

Tillman, L. (2001). Mentoring African American faculty in predominantly White institutions. *Research in Higher Education, 42*(3), 295–325.

Turner, C. (2006). Women of color in academe: Living with multiple marginality. *Journal of Higher Education, 73*(1), 74–93.

Welch, O. (1996). *An examination of effective mentoring models in the academy.* Paper presented at the Annual Meeting of the American Educational Research Association (New York City, April 8–13, 1996). EDRS ED394464 HE 029160

West, D. (2004). Group mentoring: Benefits and tensions. *Training and Development in Australia, 31*(2), 22–24.

West, M., & Curtis, J. (2006). *AAUP faculty gender equity indicators 2006.* Washington, DC: American Association of University Professors.

Wilson, P., Valentine, D., & Pereira, A. (2002). Perceptions of new social work faculty about mentoring experiences. *Journal of Social Work Education, 38*(2), 317–333.

Wingard, D., Garman, K., & Reznik, V. (2004). Facilitating faculty success: Outcomes and cost benefit of the UCSD National Center of Leadership in Academic Medicine. *Academic Medicine, 79*(10), 9–11.

Wunsch, M. (Ed.) (1994). Mentoring revisited: Making an impact on individuals and institutions. *New Directions for Teaching and Learning, 57.* San Francisco: Jossey-Bass.

Zafar, M., Roberts, K., & Behar-Horenstein, L. (2012). Mentoring perceptions and experiences of culturally diverse tenure-accruing faculty. *Florida Journal of Educational Administration & Policy, 5*(2), 58–67.

Zahorski, D. (2002). Nurturing scholarship through holistic faculty development: A synergistic approach. *New Directions for Teaching and Learning, 90,* 29–37.

Zellers, D., Howard, V., & Barcie, M. (2008). Faculty mentoring programs: Reenvisioning rather than reinventing the wheel. *Review of Educational Research, 78*(3), 552–588.

Appendices

The forms supplied in the following appendices are also available as free downloads at www.Styluspub.com/Books/BookDetail.aspx?productID=391687.

APPENDIX A: Books and Web Resources 59

APPENDIX B: Relationship-Building Exercises 65
    Relationship-Building Tasks and Ice Breakers, 65
    Questions for Building Relationships and Conducting Positive Check-In, 67
    Suggestions on Leading a Balanced Life as an Academic, 69

APPENDIX C: Active Mentoring Worksheets 71
    Needs Assessment for New Faculty, 72
    Common Pitfalls for New Faculty Members, 73
    Taking Control of Your E-Mail, 74
    Work Habits: Strengths and Areas to Strengthen, 75
    Reminisce for a Moment, 76

APPENDIX D: Closure Activities 77
    Closure or Positive Summary Tasks, 77
    Dear Mentoring Group or Mentor, 78
    Summary of What You Have Learned About Preparing for Tenure, 79

APPENDIX E: Group Mentoring Materials 81
    Group Facilitator Training Outline for Agenda, 81
    Format for Mentoring Groups, 81
    Guidelines for Facilitating Groups, 82
    Planning Template for Mentoring Group Session, 83
    Mentoring Group Contract, 84
    Analysis of Your Mentoring Group Session, 85
    Assessment for a Mentoring Group or Individual Mentoring, 86

APPENDIX F: Program Implementation Materials 87
    Application for the New Faculty Mentoring Program, 88
    Signature Page: Mentee Clearance With Department Chair and Dean, 91
    Signature Page: Mentor Clearance With Department Chair and Dean, 92
    New Faculty Mentoring Program Mentor Orientation: Short Version, 93
    New Faculty Mentoring Program Mentee Orientation, 95
    New Faculty Mentoring Program Statement of Commitment and Confidentiality, 97

APPENDIX G: Program Assessment Materials   99
    New Faculty Mentoring Program Final Evaluation,   100
    New Faculty Mentoring Program Follow-up Questionnaire,   105

APPENDIX H: Department-Level Materials   107
    Departmental Mentoring Checklist,   108
    Time Commitment for Faculty Senate Committees,   110
    Possible Tasks for a Graduate Assistant,   111
    Five-Year Tenure Preparation Plan,   112

APPENDIX I: Sample Program Documents   117
    Job Description: Director, New Faculty Mentoring Program,   118
    University- or School-Level Survey of Current Departmental Practice
      With New Faculty,   119
    Mentor Training Agenda for a Three-Hour Session,   120

APPENDIX A

Books and Web Resources

Faculty Life

Boice, R. (1992). *The new faculty member*. San Francisco: Jossey-Bass.

Boice, R. (2000). *Advice for new faculty members*. Boston: Allyn & Bacon.

Burnam, J. J., Hooper, L. M., & Wright, V. H. (2010). *Tools for dossier success: A guide for promotion and tenure*. New York: Routledge.

Darley, J. M., Zanna, M. P., & Roediger, H. L. (Eds.). (2003). *The compleat academic* (2nd ed.). Washington, DC: American Psychological Association.

Lang, J. M. (2005). *Life on the tenure track: Lessons from the first year*. Baltimore, MD: Johns Hopkins University Press.

Obeng, K. (2005). *Surviving academia: A guide to new professors*. Boca Raton, FL: Universal.

Robertson, D. (2003). *Making time, making change: Avoiding overload in college teaching*. Stillwater, OK: New Forums.

Seldin, P., & Miller, J. E. (2008). *The academic portfolio: A practical guide to documenting teaching, research and service*. San Francisco: Jossey Bass.

Issues in Diversity

Li, G., & Beckett, G. H. (2005). *"Strangers of the academy:" Asian women scholars in higher education*. Sterling, VA: Stylus.

Rocquemore, K. A., & Laszloffy, T. (2008). *The Black academic's guide to winning tenure—Without losing your soul*. Boulder, CO: Lynne Rienner.

Stanley, C. (2006). *Faculty of color: Teaching in predominantly White colleges & universities*. San Francisco: Jossey-Bass.

Mentoring

Carnell, E., MacDonald, J., & Askew, S. (2006). *Coaching and mentoring in higher education*. London: Institute of Education.

Cohen, N. H. (1999). *The mentees guide to mentoring*. Amherst, MA: HRD Press.

Crone, W. C. (2010). *Survive and thrive: A guide for untenured faculty*. San Rafael, CA: Morgan & Claypool.

Hunter, D. (1995). *The art of facilitation*. Cambridge: MA: DeCapo.

Jenkins, J. C., & Jenkins, M. R. (2006). *The 9 disciplines of a facilitator*. San Francisco: Jossey-Bass.

Johnson, B. (2007). *On being a mentor: A guide for higher education faculty*. Mahwah, NJ: Lawrence Erlbaum.

Zachary, L. J. (2000). *The mentor's guide*. San Francisco: Jossey-Bass.

Zachary, L. J. (2005). *Creating a mentoring culture*. San Francisco: Jossey-Bass.

Research

Bishop-Clark, C., & Dietz-Uhler, B. (2012). *Engaging in the scholarship of teaching & learning*. Sterling, VA: Stylus.

Clayton, P. H., Bringle, R. G., & Hatcher, J. A. (2012). *Research on service learning: Conceptual frameworks and assessment*. Sterling, VA: Stylus.

Cross, K. P., & Steadman, M. H. (1996). *Classroom research: Implementing the scholarship of teaching*. San Francisco: Jossey-Bass.

Davidson, C. I., Ambrose, S. A., & Simon, H. A. (1994). *The new professor's handbook: A guide to teaching & research*. San Francisco: Jossey-Bass.

Howlett, S. (2011). *Getting funded: The complete guide to writing grant proposals*. Seattle, WA: Word & Rabey.

McKinney, K. (2007). *Enhancing learning through the scholarship of teaching & learning.* San Francisco: Jossey-Bass.

Ogden, T. E., & Goldberg, I. A. (2002). *Research proposals: A guide to success* (3rd ed.). San Diego, CA: Academic Press.

Weimer, M. (2006). *Enhancing scholarly work on teaching & learning.* San Francisco: Jossey-Bass.

Teaching

Andre, R., & Frost, P. J. (Eds.). (1996). *Researchers hooked on teaching.* Thousand Oaks, CA: SAGE.

Bain, K. (2004). *What the best college teachers do.* Cambridge, MA: Harvard University Press.

Cox, M. (2004). Introduction to learning communities. *New Directions for Teaching and Learning, 97,* 5–23.

Davis, J. R., & Arend, B. D. (2013). *Facilitating seven ways of learning.* Sterling, VA: Stylus.

Fink, D. (2003). *Creating significant learning experiences.* San Francisco: Jossey Bass.

Grunert, J., Millis, B., & Cohen, M. (2008). *The course syllabus: A learning-centered approach.* (2nd ed.). San Francisco: Jossey-Bass.

Lang, J. M. (2008). *On course: A week-by-week guide to your first semester of college teaching.* Cambridge, MA: Harvard University Press.

McKeachie, W. (2013). *Teaching tips: Strategies, research, and theory for college and university teachers* (14th ed.). Belmont, CA: Cengage Learning.

Mezeske, R.J., & Mezeske, B A. (2007). *Beyond tests & quizzes.* San Francisco: Jossey-Bass.

Palmer, P. (2007). *The courage to teach* (10th ed.). San Francisco: Jossey-Bass.

Richlin, L. (2006). *Blueprint for learning: Constructing college courses to facilitate, assess and document learning.* Sterling, VA: Stylus.

Simkins, S., & Maier, M. (2009). *Just in time teaching.* Sterling, VA: Stylus.

Stanley, C. A., & Porter, M. E. (Eds.). (2001). *Engaging large classes.* San Francisco: Jossey-Bass.

Walvoord, B. E., & Anderson, V. J. (2009). *Effective grading: A tool for learning and assessment in college.* San Francisco: Jossey-Bass.

Writing

Belcher, W. L. (2009). *Writing your journal article in twelve weeks: A guide to academic publishing success.* Thousand Oaks, CA: SAGE.

Boice, R. (1990). *Professors as writers: A self-help guide to productive writing.* Stillwater, OK: New Forums Press.

Booth, V. (1993). *Communicating in science* (2nd ed.). Cambridge, UK: Cambridge University Press.

Germano, W. (2008). *Getting it published: A guide for scholars and anyone else serious about serious books* (2nd ed.) Chicago: University of Chicago Press.

Goodson, P. (2012). *Becoming an academic writer: 50 exercises for paced, productive, and powerful writing.* Thousand Oaks, CA: SAGE.

Katz, M. (2006). *From research to manuscript: A guide to scientific writing.* New York: Springer Science.

Silva, P. J. (2007). *How to write a lot: A practical guide to productive academic writing.* Washington, DC: American Psychological Association.

University/College Mentoring Programs

Websites

University	*Mentoring Program*	*Website*
University of Massachusetts	Grants to support mentoring projects at the department, interdepartmental, school/college, institutional, cross-institutional levels, and affinity groups. Mutual Mentoring Program: Encourages the development of strong, productive, and substantive mentoring networks at all stages of the academic career; special emphasis on faculty of color	http://www.umass.edu/ctfd/ mentoring/resources.shtml
Texas Tech University (3 programs)	Individual Faculty Mentoring Program: Faculty member can maintain/initiate mentorship relationship with local faculty member or faculty from another academic institution; relationship is documented and meets mentoring guidelines	http://www.ttuhsc.edu/elpaso/admin/ documents/Faculty_Mentoring_ Program.pdf
	Departmental Faculty Mentoring Program: Department chairs assign mentor from within the department to mid-/junior-level faculty member who has been hired within the last 3 years	
	Institutional Formal Faculty Mentoring Program: Outcome-driven program targeting mid-/junior-level, Hispanic, women, and other minority group faculty members within first 3 years of hiring; pairs university faculty with target faculty member for one year; renewal of relationship available upon request	
University of Minnesota	President's Emerging Leaders project: Faculty mentoring for probationary faculty; focuses on tenure process and standards as well as life/work balance and colleague collaboration; part of Collaborative on Academic Careers in Higher Education (COACHE) survey.	http://www.academic.umn.edu/ provost/faculty/pdf/PELMentor Report.pdf
University of Texas at Dallas	Goal: To assist junior faculty in developing their research, teaching, and professional skills. Website said program was for the 2009 calendar year; unsure whether it is still continuing. Participants were encouraged to develop a mentoring team, not just one mentor. Resources were made available on how to recruit experts to serve as mentors from outside the UTD campus. UTD offered workshops.	http://www.utdallas.edu/ facultymentoring/

(continues)

(continued)

University	Mentoring Program	Website
University at Albany (State University of New York)	This link is to a mentoring handbook that appears to recommend that faculty and staff engage in some type of mentoring relationship. No specifics on any formal program. Handbook did offer a lot of good information—financial benefits of mentoring, forms for mentoring relationship goals, etc.	http://www.albany.edu/academics/ mentoring.best.practices.appendices .shtml
Emory University	Passages Program: Sponsored by Provost's Office. Focused on junior faculty and pairs them with senior faculty who have achieved tenure in their school, but in a different department. The pair work on priorities, a network of advisors, increasing visibility, understanding university's culture and the tenure process. Workshops offered.	http://www.emory.edu/EMORY_ REPORT/erarchive/1999/March/ ermarch.29/3_29_99williams.html
University of California, San Diego	Goal: To help new faculty members adjust to the new environment. Department chair assigns mentor. Mentor contacts mentee before he or she arrives and meets with mentee regularly over at least the first 2 years. Relationship helps with networking, finding grants, getting acclimated, etc.	https://mentorship.ucsd.edu/Default .aspx
Stanford Medical School	Faculty mentoring program: Designed to help younger faculty plan careers. Mentee is to contact department chair and then the assigned mentor.	http://facultymentoring.stanford.edu/
University of Wisconsin	Women Faculty Mentoring Program: All newly hired and newly tenured women are invited. Untenured women are paired with tenured women in their field, but outside their department.	http://www.provost.wisc.edu/women/ mentor.html
University of Oregon	Women Faculty Resource Network Mentoring Program: Mentoring for junior women faculty to assist them in attaining their academic goals, namely tenure track. This program pairs women and offers resources for the relationship.	http://www.regender.org/reports- publications/center-study-women- society-university-oregon-women- color-borders-and-power
Harvard School of Public Health	Department-based mentoring for junior faculty and directory of junior faculty mentoring	http://www.faculty.harvard.edu/sites/ default/files/downloads/2.2.4%20 HPSH%20-%20Junior%20 Faculty%20Mentoring%20and%20 Development%20Program.pdf
Kansas State University College of Veterinary Medicine	Parallel Paths Initiative: College-level group mentoring program across career stages	http://www.vet.k-state.edu/events/ awards/teaching09.htm

University	Mentoring Program	Website
Tufts University School of Arts and Sciences	Interdepartmental mentoring program for junior faculty	http://as.tufts.edu/about/workingas/ mentoringprogram.htm
University of Toronto's Department of Physiology	Individual mentorship committees for all incoming faculty	http://www.physiology.utoronto.ca/ res/mentor.htm
Michigan State University	University-wide faculty mentoring policy implemented at college level and faculty mentoring resource center	http://www.adapp-advance.msu.edu/ faculty-mentoring-resource-center
University of Rhode Island	University-wide faculty mentoring policy implemented at college level and mentoring resources	http://www.uri.edu/advance/ faculty_development/mentor_ training_program.html
University of Virginia	Faculty mentoring initiative connects junior faculty with mentors outside of their department	http://trc.virginia.edu/Resources/ Mentoring/Faculty_Mentoring_ Initiative.htm
Drexel University	Career development awards to establish national or international networks outside of institution	http://www.drexel.edu/fde/ CDAOverview.html
Case Western Reserve	"Hotline Coaching" for all women faculty	http://www.case.edu/admin/aces/ hotline.html
Connecticut College	Johnson Seminar provides peer mentoring for incoming faculty	http://www.conncoll.edu/offices/ center-for-teaching--learning/ ctl-programs/class-of-57 -teaching-seminar/
University of Illinois	Junior Faculty Mentoring: New tenure-track faculty are paired with mentors from outside their home departments who share a common research interest or whose disciplines are related. Mentors provide helpful advice on time management, working with Teaching Assistants, and working with students with academic problems/personal crises. Program is optional	http://www.las.illinois.edu/faculty/ services/academy/programs/ mentoring/
University of North Carolina–Chapel Hill	Pharmacy department received endowment to begin program focusing on recruitment and retention (promotions and tenure) and using unique experiences of existing faculty. Program is voluntary, and mentoring teams meet weekly.	http://www.pharmacy.unc.edu/ faculty/bill-and-karen-campbell- faculty-mentoring-program

(continues)

(continued)

University	Mentoring Program	Website
Indiana University	Program sponsored by the Department of Curriculum and Instruction: New faculty are assigned a mentor within the first semester of their hire. Focuses on expectations and resources for tenure and promotion. Mentors advocate and advise but are not involved in the annual evaluation of the new faculty member.	http://education.indiana.edu/about/offices/faculty/mentoring/policy-candi.html
University of Michigan	Program from the Office of the Provost. Produced a rigorous study, "Report of the Faculty Mentoring Study: The Provost's Advisory Committee on Mentoring and Community Building"	http://www.provost.umich.edu/faculty/faculty_mentoring_study/report.html

Relationship-Building Exercises

Relationship-Building Tasks and Ice Breakers

General Instructions: The task ideas listed in the following table can be used for either one-on-one mentoring or with mentoring groups, as can the sample task sheets that follow. We hope these suggestions will stimulate additional ideas about how to build a beginning relationship either with a new faculty mentee or among a group of new faculty members.

Name of Task	Instructions
Structured Disclosure Questions	Ask your mentee or group members factual and/or positive disclosure questions in an effort to get to know him or her better. Some example questions, including positive check-ins, can be found on the following page, along with job-related questions on the next sample task sheet.
Feeling Checkup	Create a task sheet with feeling words and/or faces that can be used to elicit feelings that your mentee or group members currently have regarding a particular area of their lives. At the beginning of a relationship try to focus only on positive feelings associated with an aspect of a mentee's life.
Disclosure via a Symbol	You can create a task sheet or suggest a symbol to a mentee or group to elicit more gut-level disclosure from him or her/them (e.g., If you were a color last week, or a sin, or a toy, etc., what would you have been and why?). This is a way for new faculty members to talk about their last week through a symbol that often surfaces more disclosure.
Informative Piece and Discuss	Provide your mentee or group members with an informative handout (e.g., the sample task sheet "Suggestions for Leading a Balanced Life as an Academic," this appendix) and then discuss how this material applies to him or her/them.
Daily Living Analysis	Create a task sheet where members have to disclose what a typical day involves for them. Ideally, this will then stimulate further discussion around making changes in one's daily routine to ensure progress toward tenure.
Good Times/Bad Times Graph	Have members create a graph of their lives thus far indicating when times were good and bad; mentees should disclose only as much as they are comfortable sharing. Also, this graphing can focus more on just the mentee's professional life. Ask mentee to think about what made the good times satisfying, and if he or she could use that awareness to inform ways to improve current job satisfaction.

(continues)

(continued)

Name of Task	Instructions
Identify Your Strengths and Unique Characteristics	Have mentees or group members complete a task sheet delineating their strengths and unique characteristics. Have the mentee or group members share what he or she/they wrote on this sheet and then have discussion questions that ask mentees to identify how they can use their strengths/unique attributes in their current faculty position.
Rate Various Parts of Your Current Life	Create a task sheet asking mentees to use a standard rating scale (e.g., 1 to 10) to rate various parts of their lives. It is best to focus on those aspects of mentees' current faculty positions (e.g., rate your teaching, university service, writing, external funding).

Questions for Building Relationships and Conducting Positive Check-In

Relationship-Building Questions

What has been a recent source of happiness for you?

What are you doing to maintain some balance in your life?

What has been the most satisfying part of your new faculty position?

What is the last thing you did that was fun?

What is one thing you know about yourself in terms of making sure you stay the least stressed about your work?

Who are the people (family, friends, and colleagues) in your life who are currently good sources of support for you?

What is something you still need to do to feel better about your faculty position?

Questions to Conduct Positive Check-In

What is the good news about your position/work at this university?

What aspect of your faculty position do you find particularly satisfying?

What resource(s) on this campus have you found to be of assistance to you in your work?

What have been some of the unexpected benefits of your accepting this position?

What do you wish you could do differently in your faculty position?

How have your department and chair been supportive of you as a relatively new faculty member?

What are you enjoying about living in the area?

Who are some people on this campus whom you have found to be supportive and helpful when you have questions or concerns?

How could you use some of the campus resources better to benefit you in your work and your personal life?

Potential Questions for a Mentoring Group or Mentee

1. What is your profile at this university (primary assignments/expectations)?

2. What is expected of you in terms of publications to be tenured in your department?

3. What is the current practice in your department in regard to each tenured faculty member giving all junior faculty members feedback on the junior members' yearly report and updated vita at the end of the year?

4. How do you anticipate using a graduate research assistant in your research and writing?

5. How do you typically determine during a course how your students are responding to your instructional methods (e.g., see sample of early course evaluation)?

6. Do you think an undergraduate research assistant could be of any assistance to you in your research? If yes, how would this research assistant help?

7. What are your current university service assignments?

Suggestions on Leading a Balanced Life as an Academic

- Schedule time in your daily schedule for nutritious meals, physical activities, connecting with others, having alone time, and so on.
- Take breaks from your work.
- Regularly do activities that stop you from thinking about work (reading, movies, exercise, etc.).
- Schedule time with others that involves what you define as fun and enjoyable in your free time.
- Schedule time by yourself to take care of your own needs.
- Schedule your work times, stick as much as possible to that schedule, and then give yourself permission not to work during other time periods.
- Look for models around you to see how others lead a balanced life.
- Expand your friendship circle to people outside of work (e.g., through a club or hobby).
- Plan and carry out reinforcement of self after a specific period of intense work.
- Be okay with times of doing nothing; these actually help your creative juices to flow.
- Remember, you can be really good at some things and just adequate at other things and that is okay; all that really means is that you are human!
- Put time and energy into building relationships with your colleagues.
- Remember to keep laughter and humor in your life (i.e., open up those e-mails containing great jokes or humorous views on life today).
- Set realistic work goals, keeping in mind your other priorities such as family, couple relationship, raising children, and so on.
- Maintain outside interests that are potential sources of success/satisfaction for you.
- KNOW YOURSELF! We are all different and need a unique combination of things that help us feel that we truly are leading a balanced life.

Active Mentoring Worksheets

General Instructions: The task ideas listed in the table below can be used for either one-on-one mentoring or with mentoring groups, as can the sample task sheets that follow. We hope these suggestions will stimulate additional ideas about how to assist either a new faculty mentee or a group of mentees in sharing and discussing some of the problems, concerns, or challenges they are having in their faculty position.

Name of Task	*Instructions*
Brainstorm and Discuss	Brainstorm with your mentee or as a group all the ways you can address whatever is a relevant issue for a group or mentee (e.g., develop an effective writing schedule).
Share and Discuss	Facilitators or mentors share the three worst things or the three best things they did as a new faculty member. Ask mentee or group members to share their responses to this sharing/modeling disclosure.
Handout and Discussion Questions	Provide group with a handout related to the topic (e.g., "Common Pitfalls for New Faculty Members," found in this appendix), and then present some discussion questions to the group about points on the handout.
Complete the Task Sheet and Share	Give the mentees a task sheet that asks them to take some time to reflect on an issue related to the session topic (e.g., the sample task sheet titled "Taking Control of Your E-mail," in this appendix).
Free Association and Share	Give mentees an incomplete picture and ask them to complete it either by drawing or writing on the incomplete picture about a particular relevant issue (e.g., you could use an incomplete picture of a person daydreaming to ask mentees what they find themselves thinking in regard to their time management challenges).
Checklist and Discuss	Give mentees a checklist for the topic of the session (e.g., "Work Habits: Strengths and Areas to Strengthen" in this appendix) to complete silently first. Then ask everyone to share what he or she checked off on the list.
Protective Factors From Past and Share	Ask mentees to think of protective factors (coping skills) that have helped them cope with a job-related stress in the past. An example of this type of task is the "Reminisce for a Moment" task sheet in this appendix.
Incomplete Sentences and Discuss	Give members incomplete sentences on a sheet that relate to the topic of the session (e.g., I'm planning on applying for external funding from… My concerns about this grant proposal are…). Ask members to write each sentence completion, and then have the group or mentee share the responses. Use these responses to initiate a discussion about the topic of the session.

Needs Assessment for New Faculty

Name of Faculty Member: _____ Date: _____

Instructions: Please put a check next to the two issues or areas of concern that you would most like to further discuss and/or brainstorm in this support group or with your mentor.

_____ Learning effective time management for an academic position

_____ Prioritizing expectations within my department

_____ Developing my three-year research plan

_____ Handling requirements for university-related service

_____ Getting to know resources on the campus

_____ Maintaining a balanced life as an academic

_____ Developing an effective method for writing manuscripts

_____ Engaging in relationship building with colleagues within my department

_____ Learning what to record and keep each year for my tenure dossier

_____ Dealing with challenging students and/or honor code violations

_____ Identifying and applying to potential funding sources for my research

_____ Developing my teaching philosophy

_____ Other _____

Please feel free to offer any additional comments about what you hope to obtain from this mentoring support group.

_____

_____

_____

_____

_____

Thanks for your assistance!

Common Pitfalls for New Faculty Members

Instructions: Look over the list below and put a check by those things you are currently doing that may add to your stress load.

_____ Spend too much time on university service (e.g., committees)

_____ Overprepare for teaching your classes

_____ No set time each week for doing writing and research

_____ Often do not stick to set time for writing and research

_____ Have not reviewed teaching evaluations to inform future teaching

_____ Experience teaching challenges but have not developed a strategy for addressing these concerns

_____ Reluctant to ask for assistance or help with assigned responsibilities

_____ Difficulty saying no to requests to take on more responsibilities

_____ Spend too much time on student advising

_____ Feel lonely or isolated as a new faculty member

_____ Lack of balance between personal and professional life

Taking Control of Your E-Mail

Instructions: Place a check by those strategies you need to develop or improve.

_____ Delete e-mail before reading when it is not relevant or the material is easily available elsewhere.

_____ Read and respond immediately to e-mails that require a short answer.

_____ Do not open e-mail that will require lengthy response; do these at same time every day.

_____ Create a file of common questions and answers for your students/advisees.

_____ Put e-mails into folders to find them more easily when needed.

_____ Create letter templates for common recommendation requests.

_____ Limit your time on electronic media so it does not invade your entire day.

_____ Do not respond to e-mails or answer the phone during writing time.

Work Habits: Strengths and Areas to Strengthen

Instructions: Place a check by those work habits you possess that are strengths for you.

_____ Good time management skills

_____ Good organizational skills

_____ Able to set realistic expectations of self at work

_____ Capable of saying no when realistically unable to follow through with a request

_____ Good team relationships at work generally

_____ Able to stay out of the politics of the work setting

_____ Possess appropriate assertiveness skills to use when necessary at the workplace

_____ Usually start and end work day on time

_____ Able to ask for assistance or support at work when needed

_____ Able to shut off work once you leave your office

_____ Able to find fulfilling aspects to most jobs

_____ Capable of taking mental health days when needed

_____ Able to associate with the more positive and healthier members of a work team

_____ Spend time and energy forming relationships with colleagues

_____ Support and may even plan times of celebration at the workplace

_____ Maintain self-confidence and self-worth even during stressful times at work

_____ Able to act on concerns at work rather than worrying for long periods

Reminisce for a Moment

Think of a time when your current or past job was very satisfying to you. Now list three things that were happening or were part of that time on your job that made it satisfying for you.

1. _____

2. _____

3. _____

Which of the above three things could you make a part of your current job? Make sure these are things you can control.

_____

Closure Activities

Closure or Positive Summary Tasks

General Instructions: The task ideas listed in this table can be used for either one-on-one mentoring or with mentoring groups, as can the sample task sheets that follow. We hope these suggestions will stimulate additional ideas about how to provide a positive closure to your group or with your individual mentee.

Name of Task	Instructions
A Profile of a New You	Ask mentees to complete a sheet delineating what has changed about them as a result of the group. Ask either specific questions on this sheet or pose sentence completions (e.g., As a result of this group, I . . .).
My Faculty Position Success Plan	Create a completion task sheet for mentees to determine ways they will ensure that they work toward tenure, continue to improve their teaching, develop a writing schedule, know ways to address times of high stress, etc.
Good-bye Card Completion	Have mentees complete a good-bye card to either their mentor or the group that indicates how the mentor/group has been helpful to them. See the sample of a good-bye letter/card completion following this table.
A Vision of You in 5 Years!	Have mentees complete a sheet with some details of where they want to be in 5 years. After they complete this task, ask mentees to indicate what parts of their plans they have control over.
A Meditation Just for You	Ask mentees to write out a meditation that might prove helpful in getting through tough times in the future in their new faculty position.
Brainstorm All You Have Learned From This Group!	Ask mentees to brainstorm all the things they have learned from the group experience as a way to validate the knowledge and skills they have acquired. See similar but slightly different task example in this appendix, titled Summary of What You Have Learned About Preparing for Tenure.
Compliment Cards for Everyone!	Ask each mentee to write his or her name on the top of a 3" x 5" index card and then pass all the cards around the circle so other mentees in their group can write what they have come to like about the person whose name is on the card. In the case of one-on-one mentoring, the mentor and mentee can do this same exercise by writing positive feedback to one another on their respective cards.
Facilitator/Mentor Good-bye Card	Prepare a good-bye card for each mentee indicating what growth you have seen in him or her. Ask mentees to share their reactions to their good-bye card from either their mentor or the group facilitator. Sample incomplete good-bye letter in this appendix.

Dear Mentoring Group or Mentor

Instructions: Please complete this good-bye letter to the members of your mentoring group or to your individual mentor.

Dear Mentoring Group or Mentor,

I have really enjoyed being with you/in this group because _____

_____

_____.

In particular I found you/this group helped me _____

_____

_____.

At this time I intend to follow through with my goal/plan of _____

_____

_____.

Because of this mentoring relationship/group, I am planning on continuing to obtain support as a new faculty

member from _____

_____

_____.

I hope that we _____.

Sincerely,

_____

Summary of What You Have Learned About Preparing for Tenure

Check the action items you have done and circle the ones you still need to do.

- ☐ Develop an understanding of the culture of your department and school.
- ☐ Consider and clarify the message and direction from your departmental chair.
- ☐ Carefully consider who has been successfully tenured in your department in the past and examine their accomplishments during that time.
- ☐ If you are comfortable, talk directly to tenured faculty members to elicit their advice and suggestions for initiating a successful career in your department.
- ☐ Ask to view other departmental colleagues' tenure dossier materials.
- ☐ Explore the need to apply for an internal and/or external grant.
- ☐ Ask directly how many publications you are expected to have to be considered ready for potential tenure consideration.
- ☐ Clarify what are considered acceptable forms of publication for your department (e.g., books, articles, technical reports).
- ☐ Check to see whether other colleagues are conducting research on areas similar to your own research interests; consider asking another colleague to collaborate on a research project.
- ☐ Consider preparing publications based on your doctoral dissertation data.
- ☐ Use the writing lab on campus and/or outside reviewers to read and edit your first manuscripts.
- ☐ Develop a research and writing plan that will work for you and follow it.
- ☐ Determine the usual time required for manuscript review by journals in your field.
- ☐ Consider conducting research on your teaching that addresses both your teaching and publishing service to the university.
- ☐ Give yourself planned breaks from your research and writing, but be committed to returning to your previous schedule.
- ☐ Know yourself and make sure that you consider what else you need to be tenured in addition to all the above points.

Group Mentoring Materials

Group Facilitator Training Outline for Agenda

I. Overview and Rationale for Mentoring Group
   a. Provided by trainer and includes interesting comparison data from previous year
   b. Logistical issues related to the group meeting space

II. Unique Benefits of Working With New Faculty in Groups
   a. Mentees feel validated, not alone, and teach one another coping strategies
   b. Group provides energy/enthusiasm for mentees and facilitators

III. Format/Plan for Monthly Group Sessions
   a. Relationship-building/Ice breaker task
   b. Main task for session based on issue to be focused on
   c. Closure task—asking mentees what they enjoyed or learned

IV. Relationship-Building Exercise
   a. Conduct task that could be used for this purpose with a group
   b. Process with training group what they enjoyed or can see as the rationale/value of this task for a new mentee group

V. Preparations Before or at First Session
   a. Mentoring Group Contract—provide sample
   b. Needs Assessment—provide sample
   c. Explore potential speakers based on members' needs/requests

VI. What initially attracted you to your position at this university? What positive aspects of your job keep you here?
   a. Pose each question to training group and ask people to share
   b. Process why this awareness is important when conducting these groups

VII. Brainstorm potential issues new or almost new faculty members will have to address at the onset of this new academic year.

VIII. Experienced cofacilitators from mentee group from last year share what they learned from cofacilitating this group
   a. Highlight what helped make their mentee group effective
   b. Allow members of training group to ask questions

IX. Monthly check-in sessions scheduled after each session
   a. Provide handout, "Analysis of Your Mentoring Group Session"
   b. Review this handout with members of training group

X. What other types of support can we, as group trainers, provide to best assist you with these groups?

Format for Mentoring Groups

1. Relationship-Building Exercise
2. Check-in Exercise, except first session—provide introduction to group

3. Mini Workshop or topic to be discussed based on needs assessment

4. Closure of session—ask members what they enjoyed or found helpful

Guidelines for Facilitating Groups

1. Start and end group on time

2. Always conduct relationship-building exercise(s) and be the first to disclose

3. Follow a consistent format and clarify to group

4. Maintain balanced participation (particularly with relationship-building exercise)

5. Check-in exercise is just a point in the group to see how members are doing (keep short)

6. Do not allow any one member to talk too much or too long

7. Sometimes you may have to ask a member if he or she can wait to discuss a point further with you outside the group because the issue is too involved and only relates to that member

8. Always plan and facilitate your group based on the needs of the majority of members

9. Disclose some of your own successes and problems as a new faculty member; this will enhance points you are trying to make

10. These mentoring groups should primarily become support groups for the members; be less concerned about the topics covered or mini workshops held

11. Be sure you are engaged and enjoying this time—it's contagious!

12. Never forget the value of having a sense of humor.

Planning Template for Mentoring Group Session

Group: _____

Session Number: _____ Group Phase: ◯ Initial ◯ Middle ◯ Termination

Type of Task for Group Format	Planning Needed for This Part of Format
Relationship-Building Task	Task Planned: _____ Backup Task: _____
Main Task	Task Planned: _____ Backup Task: _____
Positive Closure	Positive closure question: _____
Processing Comments	*Process group-wide on task behavior, balanced participation, energy level of group, members' engagement in session, interest level, disruptive member(s), and ongoing development of group. _____ _____ _____ _____

Mentoring Group Contract

We ask that you, as a member of this mentoring group, make the following commitment to your cofacilitators and other group members during this academic year.

1. Be on time and stay until the end of each monthly meeting.
2. Attend all meetings as scheduled; if you cannot attend a session, please contact one of the cofacilitators.
3. Participate fully in all sessions since the combination of ideas and thoughts of all members is one of the major benefits of the mentoring group.
4. Keep all disclosure shared by other members confidential.
5. Share your feelings and concerns as you become comfortable in the group. If you have a serious concern and you are not comfortable sharing it with the entire group, ask to meet with one of the cofacilitators after the group meeting.
6. Be sensitive to other members' need to share at group sessions, and monitor your amount of sharing accordingly.
7. Ask your group members for assistance when needed and try to be as specific as possible.
8. Let your group members and facilitators know how helpful this group is for you throughout this year.

_____   _____

Signature   Date

Analysis of Your Mentoring Group Session

Instructions: When cofacilitators of these mentoring groups are processing after each session, they should address the following points. You can also use the scale below to rate each aspect of your mentoring group session and compare your ratings with your cofacilitator. You might even want your group members to complete this evaluation of a session anonymously.

Excellent   5   4   3   2   1   Poor

☐ Balanced participation level among membership

☐ Tone/energy level in the group session

☐ Engagement level of most members during the session

☐ Comfort level among members in the group and with cofacilitators

☐ Cofacilitators working as a team in leading the session

☐ Cofacilitators' level of confidence in conducting this session (in terms of both the plan and conducting the session)

☐ Cofacilitators' interest and enthusiasm in conducting this session

Any issues or concerns that surfaced among the membership

_____

Parts of the session that seem to have been most effective and why

_____

Parts of the session that seem to have been least effective and why

_____

Detailed plan for changes in next session based on this processing (in terms of both the plan and how the co-facilitators conduct the session)

_____

Assessment for a Mentoring Group or Individual Mentoring

Name of Faculty Member:_____   Date:_____

Instructions: Please number the 12 topics listed below in priority order from 1 = *of most interest to you* to 12 = *of least interest to you.* This feedback will be used to determine topics for our mentoring group sessions this year.

_____ Learning effective time management for an academic position

_____ Developing realistic expectations of undergraduates

_____ Developing a three-year research program

_____ Handling requirements for university-related service

_____ Interpreting teaching evaluations/using early course evaluations

_____ Maintaining a balanced life as an academic

_____ Developing an effective method for writing manuscripts

_____ Engaging in collaborative writing/research projects

_____ Learning different peer review formats and how feedback can inform one's teaching

_____ Developing a teaching philosophy

_____ Identifying and applying to potential funding sources for research

_____ Dealing with challenging students and/or honor code violations

_____ Other _____

Please feel free to offer any additional comments about what you hope to obtain from this mentoring support group.

_____

Program Implementation Materials

Application for the New Faculty Mentoring Program

The New Faculty Mentoring Program is open to all full-time faculty in tenure-track positions at the rank of assistant professor or above who are currently incoming new appointments or in their first or second year of teaching at _____. Selection is made by the Executive Committee of the New Faculty Mentoring Program based on the faculty member's expressed needs and ability to benefit from the program. The information submitted in this application will be used for selection purposes as well as assignments to discipline-specific Learning Communities where mentees will engage with each other several times a year.

Please send

- an electronic copy of your application to _____
- the original copy of your signature page via campus mail to _____ by April _____ (applications from newly appointed faculty by June _____)

The 20____-____ Program will have an opening event at which time you will meet and create a short list of potential mentors. You do not need to make contacts concerning a mentor before this event; mentor assignments will follow promptly after the event. Please reserve the late afternoon and evening of _____ for this important required meeting. For more information, call _____.

Name _____   Academic Rank _____

Department _____   Telephone Number _____

School/College _____   E-mail _____

Number of years employed as a full-time faculty member at _____ as of May 20____: .

1. Education

Degree	Institution	Date

2. Professional History

Position	Institution	Date

3. Briefly describe your teaching experience, both current and past. If you have had no teaching experience, please state this.

4. Briefly describe the research/creative program you are implementing or wish to implement at this institution. Make the description suitable for a lay audience.

5. Describe two or three of your expected teaching needs.

6. Describe two or three of your expected research needs.

7. Briefly describe what you expect to gain by participating in this program.

8. Please discuss anything else you wish about your possible involvement in this program.

If I am selected to participate in the New Faculty Mentoring Program, I agree to participate fully in the program's activities and complete reports, projects, and documents as requested.

I will attend the Opening Retreat on _____ [attendance required].

Applicant's Signature _____   Date_____

Signature Page: Mentee Clearance With Department Chair and Dean

Year: 20_____ – 20_____

Due Date: April _____, 20_____

Applicant's Name:

Department:

To be completed and signed by the department chair and signed by the dean after both have reviewed the application:

I have met with the above faculty member regarding workload assignment for the academic year and agree to see participation in the mentoring program as equivalent to a committee assignment during the one-year Mentoring Program.

Please contact _____ if you would like more details.

Chair's Signature _____   Date _____

Dean's Signature _____   Date_____

Comments by the chair and dean are encouraged and may be attached. Please return this signature page to _____ by April _____, 20_____.

The _____is an Equal Opportunity, Affirmative Action Employer.

Signature Page: Mentor Clearance With Department Chair and Dean

Senior Faculty's Name: _____

Department: _____

To be completed and signed by the department chair and signed by the dean after they both have reviewed the application:

I have met with the above faculty member regarding workload and agree to consider mentoring as equivalent to a committee assignment during the one-year Mentoring Program.

Please contact _____ if you would like more details.

Chair's Signature _____   Date _____

Dean's Signature _____   Date _____

Comments by the chair or dean are required in a Letter of Recommendation. Please address these qualities of an effective mentor:

- highly developed interpersonal skills
- good listening skills
- willingness to spend time with a new faculty member
- motivation to participate in a mutually beneficial relationship with a new faculty member

Please return this signature page to _____.

New Faculty Mentoring Program Mentor Orientation: Short Version

1. Feedback from mentees on mentoring

2. What is effective mentoring?

   a. What are your experiences of mentoring?

   b. List one or two characteristics of an effective mentor.

3. What do you have to offer? Why did you choose to be a mentor?

4. What we know about new faculty from the research:
   a. They spend less time on scholarly writing than necessary.
   b. They overprepare for teaching.
   c. They teach defensively.
   d. They fail to meet expectations on teaching evaluations.
   e. They experience loneliness/isolation.

5. Characteristics of quick-starters:
   a. They develop work habits that reflect their goals.
   b. They write daily.
   c. They connect with faculty across campus.
   d. They prepare adequately for engaged teaching.
   e. They integrate teaching and research.

6. Other typical issues:
   a. They don't understand tenure criteria.
   b. They have problems balancing work and life.
   c. Women and faculty of color are less satisfied with the support available to them.

7. Getting started
   a. Get to know each other informally; choose areas of help from topic list
   b. Goal setting—needs assessment for achieving tenure
   c. Use one-page proposal for $500 as a part of developing an action plan

8. How often to meet?
   a. First-year faculty perhaps more frequently than second- or third-year faculty
   b. No less than once a month; more often is preferable
   c. Can include informal coffee meetings, dinner at your home
   d. Should include watching each other teach
   e. Can include events, introductions to others

New Faculty Mentoring Program Mentee Orientation

I. A look in the mirror
  A. What we know about new faculty from the research
    1. Spend less time on scholarly writing than is necessary
    2. Overprepare for teaching
    3. Teach defensively
    4. Fail to meet expectations on teaching evaluations
    5. Experience loneliness/isolation
  B. Characteristics of quick-starters
    1. Develop work habits that reflect goals
    2. Schedule writing time (several hours per week)
    3. Connect with faculty across campus
    4. Prepare adequately for engaged teaching
    5. Integrate teaching and research
  C. Other typical issues
    1. Don't understand tenure criteria
    2. Problems with work/life balance

II. Expectations and protocols
  A. Meetings with mentor
    1. Frequency and duration
      a. Once a month at a minimum (1 hour)
      b. More meetings likely in early fall
      c. May want to meet for coffee more often for less time
    2. Location
      a. Anywhere is fine
      b. Coffee shop, lunch, dinner, office, home
      c. Whatever is comfortable
    3. Initiation of contact
      a. Mentors will contact you for meetings
      b. Call or e-mail if something comes up in between
    4. Responsibility for setting the agenda
      a. Joint responsibility based on your goals
      b. Agenda may include teaching, research, tenure, work/life balance
      c. First items: goal setting, needs assessment, mini-proposal
    5. Develop guidelines for the relationship
      a. Your expectations of the mentor
      b. Your mentor's expectations of you
      c. Boundaries (particularly time)

B. What you can expect from the mentoring relationship
   1. Support and interest in you, your work, your future
   2. Advice on university culture
   3. Connections to others who might be of help to you
   4. Connections to services offered on campus
   5. Potential for classroom observation for formative purposes
   6. Confidentiality

III. Writing an action-oriented and realistic measurable goal
   A. Write one to three goals for the year that are achievable and move you toward tenure
      1. Who: you
      2. Will do what?
      3. How will you demonstrate that you've done it?
      4. Under what conditions?
      5. With what level of success?
   B. Needs Assessment
      1. What materials will you need to accomplish this goal?
      2. What skills will you need to accomplish this goal?
      3. What resources do you have in your life?
   C. What are some options for using the $500 mini-grant to aid your success?
      1. Pay an editor for manuscript or proposal
      2. Pay a student to enter data into a database
      3. Attend a workshop to learn a skill
      4. Buy lab equipment
      5. Buy teaching/research software
      6. Buy scratch-off quiz answer sheets for active team learning
      7. Others?

Final issue: Most mentees want a mentor of the same gender and ethnicity, but research shows that mixed pairs are just as successful.

New Faculty Mentoring Program Statement of Commitment and Confidentiality

Commitment

I understand that the effectiveness of the relationships developed within this program are dependent upon my commitment to attend all scheduled sessions, and I commit myself to doing so, barring illness or emergency.

Confidentiality

Subject to university policy and any applicable legal exceptions, all information disclosed within the mentoring relationship or the Learning Communities is considered to be confidential. Examples of "university policy" and/or "applicable legal exceptions" that might require information about a participant to be disclosed to third parties include situations where a participant is believed to be a danger to self or others, where a participant is in need of immediate medical attention, or where a court order or subpoena requires disclosure.

[For Faculty Mentees: I also understand that participation in the New Faculty Mentoring Program does not guarantee a successful tenure application.]

_____   _____

Participant Signature   Date

Program Assessment Materials

New Faculty Mentoring Program
Final Evaluation

To better support the needs of pretenure faculty at _____, the New Faculty Mentoring Program is conducting a survey of this year's participants. Your responses to the survey questions will be completely confidential. However, the survey is not anonymous because we would like to have the opportunity to send you a reminder e-mail if necessary. To protect confidentiality, participants' names will not be linked to their responses, and responses will be analyzed only after being grouped with those of other participants. No individuals will be identifiable in any reports derived from these data. Summarized data will be shared with the mentors and group facilitators so they may understand what you valued and how we may improve our support of new faculty.

If you have any questions, please feel free to contact _____, Director of the New Faculty Mentoring Program, at _____.

Describe the impact of your mentoring relationship, your learning community (LC), and your own effort on each of these key areas in the development of new faculty, using the provided scale (0 = *no impact* to 5 = *critical impact*).

	Mentor	LC	Self
Connected with faculty across campus	0 1 2 3 4 5	0 1 2 3 4 5	0 1 2 3 4 5
Managed time for work and life	0 1 2 3 4 5	0 1 2 3 4 5	0 1 2 3 4 5
Adequately prepared for engaged teaching	0 1 2 3 4 5	0 1 2 3 4 5	0 1 2 3 4 5
Planned research schedule	0 1 2 3 4 5	0 1 2 3 4 5	0 1 2 3 4 5
Integrated teaching and research agendas	0 1 2 3 4 5	0 1 2 3 4 5	0 1 2 3 4 5

The following questions are open-ended. Please take the time to answer fully.

Program Structure

1. In retrospect, how did the mentoring pair selection process work out for you?

2. Was the program director accessible? Did you contact him or her during the year? Was the contact helpful?

3. Was the availability of mentoring a factor in your choosing to work at this university?

Mentor Effectiveness

1. What proportion of time spent with your mentor addressed the following areas:

Teaching	
Research	
Service	
Work/life balance	
Total	100%

2. What other kinds of contacts did you have with your mentor—for example, telephone contact, e-mail, conference attendance?

3. In what ways did your mentor help you connect with new colleagues on or off campus?

4. Did you and your mentor engage in mutual observations of each other (teaching, other)? If so, was this helpful to you and how?

5. How did your mentor's advice help you in the following areas? Circle your response using the provided scale (0 = *no impact* to 5 = *critical impact*):

Campus culture	0	1	2	3	4	5
Negotiating your departmental needs	0	1	2	3	4	5
Annual review preparation	0	1	2	3	4	5
Tenure strategies	0	1	2	3	4	5
Teaching	0	1	2	3	4	5
Research	0	1	2	3	4	5
Service	0	1	2	3	4	5
Student course evaluations	0	1	2	3	4	5
Life/work balance	0	1	2	3	4	5
Self-care	0	1	2	3	4	5

6. What did you value most about your mentoring relationship?

7. Were there any unexpected outcomes of the relationship?

Learning Communities

1. Did it seem that all members of your peer learning community had equal opportunities to participate?

2. How did the cross-discipline nature of the group affect group dynamics?

3. Do you have any suggestions for the group facilitators?

4. What did you value most about the learning community?

5. Were there any unexpected benefits of being in the learning community?

Continuing Involvement

Do you hope to keep your learning community group together to meet informally next year?

Do you hope to keep up a relationship with your mentor next year?

Would you like to be part of a writing group?

Would you attend informal open house coffee hours to discuss topics of interest?

Would you attend future workshops/panel discussions on topics of interest? Check areas of interest:

- ☐ P&T process

- ☐ P&T dossier

- ☐ Avoiding academese in professional writing

- ☐ Getting your book published

- ☐ Time management

- ☐ Getting students to engage in active reading

- ☐ Other _____

Do you have any other suggestions for the director about the program?

New Faculty Mentoring Program
Follow-up Questionnaire

Please let us know how you are doing as you progress through your career.

1. What teaching successes have you had in the past year?

2. What successes have you had in your research/creative endeavors?

3. Have you received any honors or awards in the past year?

4. Have you gone up for third-year review or tenure?

5. Any other successes you can share?

APPENDIX H

Department-Level Materials

Departmental Mentoring Checklist

Instructions: Check at the left the items that you and your mentoring partner will work on this year. At the end of each semester, indicate the rating that most closely describes your evaluation of that aspect of your mentoring relationship. You may add items at the bottom of the list. Use the Comments column to clarify ratings or indicate why you did not address an item.

	Mentor	Self	Comments
General Strategies			
Oriented to department	0 1 2 3 4 5	0 1 2 3 4 5	
Negotiated your needs and responsibilities	0 1 2 3 4 5	0 1 2 3 4 5	
Annual review preparation	0 1 2 3 4 5	0 1 2 3 4 5	
Helped mentee use available resources	0 1 2 3 4 5	0 1 2 3 4 5	
Discussed visibility strategies	0 1 2 3 4 5	0 1 2 3 4 5	
Strategized service commitments	0 1 2 3 4 5	0 1 2 3 4 5	
Clarified tenure requirements	0 1 2 3 4 5	0 1 2 3 4 5	
Self-Care			
Facilitated relationship building	0 1 2 3 4 5	0 1 2 3 4 5	
Helped with time management	0 1 2 3 4 5	0 1 2 3 4 5	
Helped with work/life balance	0 1 2 3 4 5	0 1 2 3 4 5	
Encouraged self-care	0 1 2 3 4 5	0 1 2 3 4 5	
Teaching			
Addressed teaching development	0 1 2 3 4 5	0 1 2 3 4 5	
Advised on course preparation	0 1 2 3 4 5	0 1 2 3 4 5	
Addressed online course instruction	0 1 2 3 4 5	0 1 2 3 4 5	
Addressed using student course evaluations	0 1 2 3 4 5	0 1 2 3 4 5	

	Mentor	Self	Comments
Research			
Planned research schedule (5-year plan)	0 1 2 3 4 5	0 1 2 3 4 5	
Targeting journals	0 1 2 3 4 5	0 1 2 3 4 5	
Writing and editing guidance and scheduling	0 1 2 3 4 5	0 1 2 3 4 5	
Proposal writing	0 1 2 3 4 5	0 1 2 3 4 5	
Developing collaborations	0 1 2 3 4 5	0 1 2 3 4 5	
Integrated teaching and research agendas	0 1 2 3 4 5	0 1 2 3 4 5	

Time Commitment for Faculty Senate Committees

Name of Committee	*Average Time Commitment*
Elected Committees	
Senate	High
Committee on Due Process	Medium to High
Faculty Grievance	Medium
Faculty Assembly Delegation	High
Faculty Government	Medium to High
Academic Policies and Regulations	Medium to High
Committee on Committees	Low
Faculty Promotions and Tenure Guidelines Committee	Medium to High
Graduate Studies Committee	Medium
Research Grants Committee	High
Undergraduate Curriculum Committee	High
Appointed Committees	
Academic Computing	Low
Budget Committee	Medium
Enrollment Management Committee	High
Faculty Compensation Committee	Medium
Faculty Professional Development and Welfare Committee	Medium
Intercollegiate Athletics Committee	Medium to High
Research Policies Committee	Medium to High
University Teaching and Learning Center Committee	Medium
General Education Council	High
Scholarly Communication Committee	Medium

Key to time commitment rating

Low: One to two meetings per year with workload done by members

Medium: Monthly meetings for approximately one hour

High: Monthly meetings for approximately two hours and additional assignments to complete each month

Possible Tasks for a Graduate Assistant

Research

Create an Excel file to keep track of all your IRB proposals with a notebook system

Transcription of interviews or focus groups

Data organization

Pull articles for a review of the literature

Put articles into endnote

Data analysis

Teaching

Follow the Discussion Board in Blackboard for student questions

Grade assignments

Proctor exams

Service

Newsletters

Organize reviews you may be doing

Technology

Learn how to do something you need to learn and teach you how to do it

Load software onto a new computer

Review

Create a reappointment notebook

Create tenure notebooks

Five-Year Tenure Preparation Plan

Name of Faculty Member: _____

Indicate timeline for this five-year plan: _____

Department Affiliation: _____ School: _____

Number of accepted publications expected in this period: _____

Number of already accepted/published articles/books counted for this timeline: _____

Indicate study data completely collected for potential manuscript(s): _____

_____

_____

Indicate study currently being set up for potential manuscript(s): _____

_____

_____

Indicate any potential funding sources for research: _____

_____

_____

Indicate any potential collaborations for current or future research: _____

_____

_____

Do you have study findings that could be used for more than one publication? If yes, indicate which one and the general focus of each article.

_____

_____

_____

Year One of Five-Year Tenure Preparation Plan

Academic Year: _____

Number of manuscripts expected to complete this year and submit for publication: _____

Focus or title of anticipated publication(s): _____

_____

Potential journals or publishers for manuscript submission:

_____

Dates of manuscripts submitted: _____

Number of manuscripts accepted for publication with dates: _____

_____

_____

Year Two of Five-Year Tenure Preparation Plan

Academic Year: _____

Number of manuscripts expected to complete this year and submit for publication: _____

Focus or title of anticipated publication(s): _____

_____

Potential journals or publishers for manuscript submission: _____

_____

Dates of manuscripts submitted: _____

Number of manuscripts accepted for publication with dates: _____

_____

_____

Year Three of Five-Year Tenure Preparation Plan

Academic Year: _____

Number of manuscripts expected to complete this year and submit for publication: _____

Focus or title of anticipated publication(s): _____

_____

Potential journals or publishers for manuscript submission: _____

_____

Dates of manuscripts submitted: _____

Number of manuscripts accepted for publication with dates: _____

_____

_____

Year Four of Five-Year Tenure Preparation Plan

Academic Year: _____

Number of manuscripts expected to complete this year and submit for publication: _____

Focus or title of anticipated publication(s): _____

_____

Potential journals or publishers for manuscript submission: _____

_____

Dates of manuscripts submitted: _____

Number of manuscripts accepted for publication with dates: _____

_____

_____

Year Five of Five-Year Tenure Preparation Plan

Academic Year: _____

Number of manuscripts expected to complete this year and submit for publication: _____

Focus or title of anticipated publication(s): _____

_____

Potential journals or publishers for manuscript submission: _____

_____

Dates of manuscripts submitted: _____

Number of manuscripts accepted for publication with dates: _____

_____

Total number of manuscripts published in five-year period: _____

Total number of manuscripts accepted but not yet published: _____

Total number of manuscripts still under review: _____

Number of potential future manuscripts based on exiting data: _____

Sample Program Documents

Job Description: Director, New Faculty Mentoring Program

This description is for a half-time position. The New Faculty Mentoring Program provides support for the mentors as well as for the group facilitators for ____ learning communities. The Learning Communities comprise six to seven new faculty members and are facilitated by two senior faculty members. The group facilitators also have a learning community facilitated by the director. The mentors are divided into three learning communities as well, with the director as the facilitator.

Duties in this role include:

Planning and Development

- development of the program
- development of application materials, fliers, and brochures
- recruitment of participants
- presentations to faculty and chairs in various schools and the college
- ongoing website development
- development of training for mentors and group facilitators
- presentations at faculty development conferences

Coordinating of Program Events

- coordinating group meeting schedules for learning communities
- matching mentees with mentors
- monthly meetings with group facilitation expert for ongoing planning of training for group facilitators
- coordination with Alumni Office to recruit manuscript readers from retired faculty
- regular meetings with advisory committee
- monthly meetings with mentor and group facilitator learning communities
- planning opening and closing events
- planning monthly workshops/coffee hour discussions
- development of writing groups for new faculty participants
- development and administration of assessment materials, including

  - first-semester phone calls to all participants
  - second-semester focus groups
  - questionnaires

- Coordination of mentee proposals for mini-grants

Budgeting

- budget management with support staff
- management of $500 mini-grants for mentees
- development of a library of resources for new faculty

University- or School-Level Survey of Current Departmental Practice With New Faculty

1. As a new faculty member within my department, I was given
   ☐ orientation   ☐ mentoring   ☐ occasional meeting with chair   ☐ none of these

2. Material orientation to the department (copier, supplies, mailboxes, etc.) was given to me by:
   ☐ office staff   ☐ another professor   ☐ mentor   ☐ chair   ☐ no one

3. Structural orientation to the department (who does what, where to go for) was given to me by:
   ☐ office staff   ☐ another professor   ☐ mentor   ☐ chair   ☐ no one

4. Functional orientation to the department (faculty meetings, annual review, tenure process, etc.) was given to me by:
   ☐ office staff   ☐ another professor   ☐ mentor   ☐ chair   ☐ no one

5. Help with my teaching was given to me by:
   ☐ center for teacher learning   ☐ another professor   ☐ mentor   ☐ chair   ☐ no one   ☐ other

6. Help with my research was given to me by:
   ☐ Office of Research   ☐ another professor   ☐ mentor   ☐ chair   ☐ no one   ☐ other

7. Advice on meeting service requirements was given to me by:
   ☐ another professor   ☐ mentor   ☐ chair   ☐ no one   ☐ other

8. Advice on balancing work/life was given to me by:
   ☐ another professor   ☐ mentor   ☐ chair   ☐ no one   ☐ other

Mentor Training Agenda for a Three-Hour Session

What is effective mentoring?

Who has had a good experience of being mentored?

How many of you have been a mentor before?

What are the characteristics of a good mentor or an effective mentoring relationship?

- Good listening is key.
- Understand the overall situation of the mentee.
- Provide a sense of support and encouragement.
- Help the mentee recognize the questions to ask and where to find the answers.
- Be willing to point out what new faculty should NOT be doing.
- Open up to the mentee about your own stressors.

Why did you choose to become a mentor (think-pair-share activity)?

What do you have to offer new faculty?

- You know the culture of the institution, school, or department.
- You have been where they are.
- You are able to reframe an issue in a larger context.
- You have experience in setting goals and prioritizing.
- You understand the tenure process and, perhaps, the tenure criteria.
- You have experience with student course evaluations!

What are the characteristics of new faculty (Boice, 1990)?

- Spend less time on scholarly writing than necessary
- Overprepare for teaching
- Teach defensively
- Fail to meet expectations on teaching evaluations
- Experience loneliness/isolation
- Imposter syndrome

What are the characteristics of quick starters?

- Develop work habits that reflect goals
- Write multiple times a week
- Connect with faculty across campus
- Prepare adequately for engaged teaching
- Integrate teaching and research

What are the needs of new faculty?

- To feel connected to others and the larger institution
- Help with time management—prioritizing writing!
- Managing the balance of teaching and research
- Managing the balance of work and home life
- Editorial help with their writing

Areas in which a mentor can actively help

- Reading manuscripts, monographs, chapters
- Reading grant proposals
- Planning goals
- Writing a teaching philosophy
- Writing a research narrative
- Preparing a portfolio
- Making connections on and off campus

Areas for discussion

- Time management and work/life balance
- Prioritization process
- Student course evaluations
- Campus culture
- Negotiating with department chair
- Dealing with student problems
- Annual review
- How to use a graduate assistant

Stages of the Mentoring Relationship

Opening Stage

- Get to know your mentee—don't rush into business first
- Talk about expectations, be clear about limits
- Mentor makes first contact and sets up first few meetings
- Responsibility for contact shifts to mentee by second semester
- Define goals; they may need help here—use a checklist (handout)
- Discuss confidentiality

Issue of confidentiality

- May want to sign a confidentiality agreement
- A mentor who ends up on tenure committee may want to recuse himself or herself
- More difficult issue for within-department mentor
- More opportunity for formative assessments
- Avoid summative assessments

How often to meet

- First-year faculty perhaps more frequently than second or third year
- No less than once a month
- Can include informal coffee meetings, dinner at your home
- Should include watching each other teach
- Can include events, introductions to others

Development Stage

- Ask what they need from you
- A listener
- Accountability?
- Teaching observation, formative review
- Reader for manuscripts, grant proposals, workshop proposals
- Can use a needs assessment checklist

Stay focused on goals

- When they come to you with a new "opportunity," ask whether it fits in with their current goals and whether it will help them get tenure
- Plan everything strategically
- Three-year plan
- Service responsibilities

Help them to make connections

- With services available to them on campus
- With information
- With other faculty
- With community contacts if appropriate

Independence

- Expect need to decrease over time
- Connections become infrequent
- Relationship becomes that of colleagues

The importance of good listening (activity instructions)

- Pair off
- Choose someone you don't know
- Five minutes each to talk about something
- No response except nonverbal
- Then switch

Mentoring Inside and Outside Your Department

Mentoring inside the department: Advantages?

- Know the field
- Know the departmental culture
- Know the journals
- Know what tenure expectations are (usually)
- Know the students
- May be able to collaborate on research

Mentoring inside the department: Disadvantages?

- Insularity of staying within department
- No one to talk with about departmental politics
- Issues of formative versus summative assessment
- Mentee can't be as frank about issues with someone who will vote on tenure

Mentoring outside the department: Advantages?

- Ability to be frank with each other
- Can read manuscripts for clarity and other issues without getting lost in the concepts
- Can offer a broader perspective on issues
- Can offer connections across campus
- Can offer formative rather than summative assessment

Mentoring outside the department: Disadvantages?

- Usually no direct aid on research
- Do not know departmental culture, tenure requirements, etc.
- Could make suggestions that aren't appreciated inside the department
- Mentoring small groups of new faculty

Who mentors the mentors?

- If there is more than one mentor here from an institution
- Plan to get together monthly to talk
- Take advantage of the collective wisdom of the group
- Develop a mentoring culture

Benefits of Mentoring

- Reduced stress
- Satisfaction with the institution
- Professional confidence and identity
- Networking
- Professional skill development
- Productivity

Bibliography for Training Session

Boice, R. (1990). *Professors as writers: A self-help guide to productive writing.* Stillwater, OK: New Forums.

Boice, R. (1992). *The new faculty member: Supporting and fostering professional development.* San Francisco: Jossey-Bass.

Huang, C. A., & Lynch, J. (1995). *Mentoring: The Tao of giving and receiving wisdom.* New York: HarperCollins.

Palmer, P. J. (1998). *The courage to teach: Exploring the inner landscape of a teacher's life.* San Francisco: Jossey-Bass.

Robertson, D. R. (2003). *Making time, making change: Avoiding overload in college teaching.* Stillwater, OK: New Forums.

Schoenfeld, A. C., & Magnan, R. (1994). *Mentor in a manual: Climbing the academic ladder to tenure.* Madison, WI: Atwood Publishing.

Silvia, P. (2007). *How to write a lot.* Washington, DC: APA Books.

Zachary, L. J. (2000). *The mentor's guide.* San Francisco: Jossey-Bass.

About the Authors

SUSAN L. PHILLIPS developed the New Faculty Mentoring Program for The University of North Carolina at Greensboro (UNCG) and served as the director for five years. Through this process she has learned that mentoring not only affects a new faculty member's progress toward tenure, but also develops a strong sense of community and connection to the university, a key factor in faculty retention. Susan has conducted regional and national workshops on mentoring and the tenure process at Lilly Conferences, the POD Conference, and conferences for doctoral students. In addition, she has published articles on mentoring in *Journal of Excellence in College Teaching* and *The Department Chair*. At UNCG since 1999, Susan is an associate professor of audiology in the Department of Communication Sciences and Disorders. She has an active teaching load and research agenda, which includes National Institutes of Health–funded projects. She received her doctorate from the University of Maryland at College Park.

SUSAN T. DENNISON has an MSW degree and is an associate professor in the Department of Social Work at UNCG, where she has been on faculty for 20 years. She has an active teaching and research program at UNCG with external funding at both the state and foundation levels. Susan's expertise, teaching, and research have focused on group work for the past 30 years resulting in nine books and numerous articles. She ran a national group consulting company and presented at both national and international conferences on group work. Susan is an ongoing consultant and trainer for the UNCG Faculty Mentoring Program. As a result of her work on this mentoring project, she coauthored an article and presented at Lilly South. Susan has come to believe that faculty mentoring programs can not only retain minority faculty but also change the entire culture of a university.

Index

administrators, 2–3
  guidelines for, 35–39
  support of, 49
assessment
  of departmental mentoring, 33–34
  feedback as, 32
  mentoring program, 30, 41–42, 46, 51
  self-, new faculty, 24–25

Boice, B., 6, 51–52
Boyle, P., 51–52

Clutterbuck, D., 47
collegial relationship, 8
Collins, T., 48
communication style, 22
competition, 9
contracts, 18
costs
  mentoring program, 42, 51
  recruitment, 2, 48
Cox, M., 11, 51
Curtis, P., 52

Dennison Group Practice model
  cohesion in, 13
  framework for, 11–14
  group goals attainment in, 15
  group values in, 14
  guidelines, 11–18
  initial phase in, 12–15
  "in vivo" learning in, 17
  mentor involvement in, 15–16
  mentor modeling in, 17–18
  middle phase in, 12–16
  without middle phase movement, 15–16
  participation balance in, 16–17
  planning in, 17

process and targeting goals in, 13–15
process and targeting goals variety in, 14–15
process goals, 11–15
process goals attainment in, 14
relationship-building tasks in, 16
session format in, 17
targeted group goals in, 12–13, 15
termination phase in, 12–15
timing in, 12
trust building in, 16
variety in, 17
department, 7
  administration set up guidelines for, 3
  culture of, 6, 9, 27–28
departmental mentoring
  assessment of, 33–34
  benefits of, 30–31
  challenges of, 31–32
  formal, importance of, 27–28
  inter versus intra, 5–6, 8–9, 22
  logistics of, 28–30
  principles of, 28
  professional development stages in, 32–33
Detmar, K., 48
Duane, J., 47

ethnicity, 2
  cultural competency and, 50
  department value of, 27
  in group mentoring, 18
  mentor match of, 29, 31, 50, 52
evaluation. *See* assessment

faculty retirement, 1–2, 48

gender
  department value of, 27
  in group mentoring, 18

mentor match of, 29, 31, 50, 52–53
Girves, J., 51
gratitude, 25
group mentoring, 38. *See also* Dennison Group
        Practice model
    cross-disciplinary, 24
    gender in, 18
    individual mentoring and, 3, 50
    Learning Communities as, 11
    participation in, 24
group mentoring guidelines, 3
    for facilitating, 19–20
    group size in, 18–19
    modeling in, 20
    for planning, 19
    scheduling, 13
    setting up, 18–19
guidelines, 1, 3
    for administrators, 35–39
Gwathmey, J., 51

humility, 5
Hutinger, J., 51

Institutional Review Board (IRB) application, 46
interdepartmental versus intradepartmental
        mentoring, 5–6, 8–9, 22

Lane, G., 47
Learning Communities, 11
listening, 5
literature review, 3
    faculty mentoring value, 47–49
    logistics for success, 49–51
    mentoring program benefits, 51–52
    mentoring program challenges, 52–53
logistics
    of departmental mentoring, 28–30
    for success, 49–51
    for university-wide mentoring program, 36–37
Lumpkin, A., 51

meetings, 46
    agenda for, 8
    goals in, 9
    meet-and-greet, 45
    of mentors and facilitators, 45–46
    orientation, 45
    preparation for, 9

questions for, 7
    time for, 23, 31, 50–51
mentees. *See* new faculty
mentoring
    definition, 47
    recognition for, 10, 50
    from self, 9
mentoring program
    assessment, 30, 41–42, 46, 51
    benefits from, 1–2, 21–22, 30–31, 51–52
    coordination of, 49–50
    feedback on, 32
    monitoring of, 29–30
    orientation, 45
    policy for, 28, 32
    proposal development, 41–43
    university-wide one-on-one, 37–38
    website for, 42
mentoring program director, 3
    implementation, 43–46
    proposal development, 41–43
mentor relationship, 16
    collegial, 8
    holistic, 6
    intradepartmental, 5–6, 8–9, 22
    mutual respect in, 5
    parameters setting in, 7
    safe space in, 5
    stages of, 7–8
mentors
    assistance areas for, 6
    characters of, 5–6
    communication style of, 22
    facilitator meetings with, 45–46
    former, 23–24
    humanity of, 5
    humility of, 5
    as listener, 5
    mentors for, 10
    modeling of, 17–18, 20
    offerings of, 6
    perspectives of, 5
    recruitment of, 43–44
    rewards for, 10
    selection of, 3, 9, 22–23, 28–29
    strategies for, 2–3
    team of, 18
    tenure and, 22
    training for, 44–45

trust of, 5
variety of, 22
Mertens, D., 51
minorities. *See* ethnicity
modeling, 17–18, 20
Mullen, C., 51

needs assessment, 23, 41–42
new faculty, 2
   characteristics of, 6–7
   concerns of, 1
   expectations, 23–24
   gratitude, 25
   group participation, 24
   needs of, 3, 7, 9, 19, 21–22
   personal questions about, 7
   questions to, 7
   self-assessment, 24–25
   stress of, 21
   writing time of, 9–10

Okawa, G., 50

Palmer, P., 9
Parson, A., 47
Phillips, S., 53
planning
   in Dennison Group Practice model, 17
   group mentoring guidelines for, 19

quick starters, 6–7, 21

race. *See* ethnicity
recruitment
   costs of, 2, 48
   of mentors, 43–44

Sands, R., 47
selection, mentor, 3, 9
   qualities for, 28–29
   speed meet for, 22–23
self-assessment, 24–25
set up guidelines, 3, 18–19
Sorcinelli, M., 28
Stanley, C., 50
stress, 21

support, 49
   levels, for university-wide mentoring program,
      38–39
   university-wide mentoring program logistics,
      36–37
surveillance, 9

tenure, 2, 22
Thomas, D., 52
time
   for meeting, 23, 31, 50–51
   of mentor match, 29, 50–51
   setting up group mentoring and, 18–19
   for writing, 9–10, 23
trust, 5
Turner, C., 50

unit-level mentoring programs, 38
university-wide mentoring program
   advantages, 35–36
   alternative program models, 37–38
   assessment, 46
   challenges, 39
   implementation, 43–46
   logistical support, 36–37
   needs assessment for, 41–42
   pilot test for, 43
   recruitment for, 43–44
   resources for, 42
   stakeholder concerns, 41
   support levels for, 38–39
   sustainability, 36–37

Welch, O., 50
West, M., 52
writing
   editors for, 42
   time for, 9–10, 23
Wunsch, M., 47

Yalom, E., 11
Yoshinaga-Itano, C., 31

Zellers, D., 51, 53
Zepeda, Y., 51

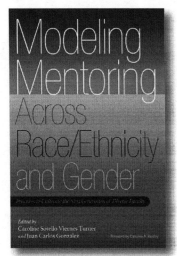